Special Praise for

THE JAGUAR MAN

"*The Jaguar Man* does the seemingly impossible—weave a beautiful tale out of a horrific experience. Lara Naughton inspires and uplifts even as she shares difficult truths. This book will encourage you to reimagine—and believe in—your own capacity for compassion, courage, and resilience."

—**KELLY McGONIGAL, PhD,** BESTSELLING AUTHOR OF
The Upside of Stress AND *The Willpower Instinct*

"*The Jaguar Man* is less a story than a slap. It is an intensely lyrical expression of darkness, of pain, of an ugly act of violence that becomes transformational. Inspiring and written in spare, completely original, painfully honest, magical, hammering prose, this book is not to be missed."

—**MARK BOWDEN,** THE NEW YORK TIMES BESTSELLING AUTHOR
OF *Black Hawk Down*

"What a privilege it has been for me to be part of Lara's journey. And to now see her harrowing experience transmuted into a sojourn of healing and love described so vulnerably, so sublimely in this book, I can only describe *The Jaguar Man* and its author as a blessing to the world."

—MICHAEL BERNARD BECKWITH, AUTHOR OF *Spiritual Liberation*

"Lara Naughton has rewritten the survivor narrative into a radical poetics that challenges all of our ideas about sexual and spiritual trauma. At the heart of this story is a kidnapping and violence against the body and spirit of a woman deep in the Belize tropics. But her journey is not into the heart of darkness. The darkness is rewritten as a kind of portal, and language is reinvented as the mode by which we can reinvent ourselves, even in the face of brutality. Like Roxane Gay's novel *An Untamed State*, we are given the story of violence unflinchingly, and yet beauty still rises like a hymn to the body, bringing the soul back home."

—LIDIA YUKNAVITCH, BESTSELLING AUTHOR OF
The Small Backs of Children AND *The Chronology of Water*

"A marvelous book written with the deft hand of a journalist and told with the grip of an old fashioned storyteller. The magic of this book is not so much that Lara Naughton had to reach deep into a cauldron of wit and courage to survive an ordeal from a vicious, twisted villain, but rather that her redemption created a new level of understanding and wisdom that she embraced, so that she might live long enough to share this wisdom with others. That is why we read books. And that is why this is an excellent one."

—JAMES MCBRIDE,
NATIONAL BOOK AWARD-WINNING AUTHOR OF *The Good Lord Bird*

"*The Jaguar Man* is a terribly beautiful book. It will remind you of what human beings are capable of at their worst, but more importantly, it will remind you of the human capacity to survive and thrive despite unimaginable challenges. I highly recommend it."

—**KEVIN POWERS,** BESTSELLING AUTHOR OF *The Yellow Birds*

"*The Jaguar Man* is an astonishing story of how compassion and unconditional love can create reality—even change reality—beyond what our rational minds can understand. If you ever had any doubts about that, read this book."

—**KRISTIN NEFF, PhD,** AUTHOR OF
Self-Compassion: The Proven Power of Being Kind to Yourself

"*The Jaguar Man* is a highly compelling and vulnerable story of survival, heartbreak, triumph, and hope. Poignantly written, Lara Naughton shines a very bright light on what it means to live with compassion, courage, and heart."

—**CHRIS GROSSO,** AUTHOR OF *Indie Spiritualist* AND *Everything Mind*

"Revelatory in its wisdom, startling in its beauty, *The Jaguar Man* is an empowering reminder that—however daunting the path might seem—we are our own best healers. A truly vital read."

—**STEPHANIE ELIZONDO GRIEST,** AUTHOR OF
Mexican Enough: My Life between the Borderlines

"*The Jaguar Man* offers a profound and personal exploration of the impact of violent crime on survivors, their families, and communities. Naughton offers a perspective of pain, hope, healing, and redemption that is a must read for anyone who has endured trauma or loss."

—**ANNE SEYMOUR,** NATIONAL CRIME VICTIM ADVOCATE

The
JAGUAR
MAN

The
JAGUAR
MAN

A Memoir

LARA NAUGHTON

CENTRAL RECOVERY PRESS

Las Vegas

Central Recovery Press (CRP) is committed to publishing exceptional materials addressing addiction treatment, recovery, and behavioral healthcare topics.

For more information, visit www.centralrecoverypress.com.

Publisher: Central Recovery Press
3321 N. Buffalo Drive
Las Vegas, NV 89129

21 20 19 18 17 16   1 2 3 4 5

Library of Congress Cataloging-in-Publication Data

Names: Naughton, Lara.
Title: The jaguar man / Lara Naughton.
Description: Las Vegas, NV: Central Recovery Press, 2016. | Description based on print version record and CIP data provided by publisher; resource not viewed.
Identifiers: LCCN 2015051474 (print) | LCCN 2015048730 (ebook)
ISBN 9781942094210 (ebook) | ISBN 9781942094203 (paperback)
Subjects: LCSH: Naughton, Lara—Travel—Belize. | Rape victims--Belize--Biography. Americans—Belize—Biography. | Survival—Belize. | Rape victims—Psychology. Victims of violent crimes—Rehabilitation. | Compassion. | Healing.
BISAC: BIOGRAPHY & AUTOBIOGRAPHY / Personal Memoirs.
BODY, MIND & SPIRIT / Healing / General. | RELIGION / Buddhism / General (see also PHILOSOPHY / Buddhist).
Classification: LCC HV6569.B42 (print) | LCC HV6569.B42 N38 2016 (ebook)
DDC 362.883092--dc23
LC record available at http://lccn.loc.gov/2015051474

Photo of Lara Naughton by Monika Abercauph

Publisher's Note: This book contains general information about compassion and healing from sexual assault. The information is not medical advice. This book is not an alternative to medical advice from your doctor or other professional healthcare provider.

This is a memoir—a work based on fact recorded to the best of the author's memory. Our books represent the experiences and opinions of their authors only. Every effort has been made to ensure that events, institutions, and statistics presented in our books as facts are accurate and up-to-date. To protect their privacy, the names of some of the people, places, and institutions in this book may have been changed or omitted.

Cover design and interior design and layout by Marisa Jackson

O N E

He's a talker, the angry man, talks the whole time. Talks as he picks me up in his pretend cab, talks as he turns the wrong way toward Maya Beach instead of toward town, talks as he extends his hand with a knife. He tells a winding story about his son who was taken from him, his ex-wife who he hates and loves, the government on his back, a $10,000 fine for holding a joint. He considered killing himself this morning, he needs money, my money, he's going to take my money, he's going to take other things from me too, his knife is in charge, he has to get home, he can't live without his son.

I've always been a good listener, so while he traps me in the jungle beside the Caribbean Sea and brutishly inserts me into his story, I listen to him carefully, hoping to find clues about how to get out of this alive. His story isn't hard to follow, but it shifts. One madness becomes another until it takes a turn down a dark dirt road in Maya Beach. There it splinters in kaleidoscopic bits of me, him, me, him, me, him, with pieces of both of us sprinkled over sand and sea.

That night I believe what he tells me. Now I'm not sure. Maybe he told the truth about himself, maybe he lied, there's no way to know, and what does it matter? That night he says what he says, he does what he does, and I respond, my own fragments of the story turning and turning in the kaleidoscope's jewel-cut eye.

On the morning of the angry man, I'm on vacation in Belize on a peaceful Caribbean beach. The air tastes like salt. Warm air surrounds me with thick arms, and I welcome its insistent embrace. This isn't my life in Los Angeles. Here I'm relaxed, unhurried. The breeze is slow, like the waves. Even the salt takes its time from the sea to my lips. Low wooden chairs with colorful chipped paint sit empty in front of rustic cabanas. One or two tourists walk the white packed sand close to the gentle water. Several Belizeans sit in the early shade of a coconut palm, one of the few trees still standing after a devastating hurricane wiped out much of the beach.

It's Sunday, the fourth day of what I think will be two weeks of bliss in this tiny village with the quick crossing from sea to lagoon, the long sidewalk officially deemed "narrowest main street in the world," no hospital, only a police substation, and a long glorious stretch of beach dotted with hibiscus and the sea's natural debris.

I'm used to my city's saturated smells, at home my senses are fine-tuned for safety, and I'm a fairly experienced traveler alert to my surroundings, but here I don't detect a scent of danger. I'm a teacher so I take advantage of holidays and summers to explore. I've interviewed theologians in South Africa, walked along the

Great Wall of China, helped organize an arts festival in Zimbabwe, followed migrating butterflies in Mexico, ridden an ostrich, and lived on a boat. I trust my instincts, choose adventures that don't carry excessive risk, after all, I'm a single woman and usually travel alone. But I also trust in people's good nature, mostly have positive encounters, and have made lasting friendships with people I met along the way. Still, it's important to be careful.

In this quiet village, I'm happy. The sun, that great dream doctor, rises; the sun, that fierce lion of love, sets; the Earth spins and spins, and I'm like an eager child, my heart wide open to whatever I'm about to find.

I've returned to fall in love with the diver I met on this same Belizean peninsula three months ago. The one who sat down uninvited at my wooden table under a thatched umbrella, bought me tall glasses of rum punch, and talked with me into the night while wind and residue of salt water tangled my hair. It rained lightly, drizzling off the fronds of the umbrella onto the sand around our chairs. It wet my skin, and despite the warm night, I shivered.

In the past I've become friends with men in other countries but never started a romance. This diver, though; he's smart and sincere, attentive and kind. We made plans to meet again the next day. By the time I left the country a week later, we had met for dinner every night, explored the peninsula together by boat, sped across the water to a soccer game in Monkey River, danced to a reggae band at the beach bar, talked, kissed, and held hands. It was sweet; he was sweet. I wasn't in love but I thought he was sweet.

I returned to Los Angeles, and we began three months of daily emails and phone calls. We were curious about each other. We played with the possibility of love. When summer break arrived, I decided to return.

Embarkment. Los Angeles.

Disembarkment. Belize City.

Back again? asks the customs official. You must like our country.

Yes.

On the morning of the angry man, I sit looking at the sea and wonder if I could adapt to living here. The diver and I are having a wonderful time, falling in love the way we hoped we would. I'm falling in love with the diver, falling in love with the village, falling in love with the sun, sand, water, air, and sky.

The diver has always lived in this paradise. He swam before he walked, blends Creole and English in a voice as smooth as deep water. His voice, my God, his voice is so soothing, even and low. Living on the water has made him calm. He slows my city pace down, and I appreciate that. What's the rush? He balances my thinking, too. I'm an analyzer; he's a simplifier. It's a relief to not get entangled in heady debates but to take in wisdom from the stories he tells me of the sea. He's a dive master and professional fisherman, spends his days exploring the coral reef. Elkhorn, brain coral, leaf coral—it's hard to name the corals because of how many there are. Fishes likewise. Groupers, snappers, marlins, barracudas, blacktip sharks, reef sharks, hammerhead sharks, and the rarely seen tiger sharks.

When strange things come to where we live, the diver says, we tend to look at them with curiosity. Same way with the fishes. Most things under the water are curious. Most will look but won't approach. We're interfering in their world, yet they won't swim away except if we swim toward them and spook them a bit.

His birthday is next week, and I'm here to celebrate. I made him a book of the emails we sent back and forth since we met, each page uniquely designed. I think I'll give him the book on his birthday. I think the weeks will be carefree. I think my biggest worry is whether I'm being foolish and naïve starting a romance with this man. I'm aware of our differences, of course I am. I'm city; he's ocean. I'm let's make a plan; he's let's see how it goes. I live inside art, theatre, and books. He lives in an underwater galaxy I've barely touched floating on the surface. He doesn't mind our difference in age or culture or race and neither do I. I've been through enough disappointing relationships to take a chance on this sweet younger man. Last night sitting on the beach, he told me he thinks we can be happy together for a very long time.

There are dangers in scuba diving, the diver says. You should be aware of the risks, but if you're careful and follow instructions, it's a very safe sport. Don't put on scuba gear immediately. First you should learn basic skills.

There were warning signs I missed.
There are warning signs I miss.

After my first trip to Belize, I returned to Los Angeles to a swarm of bees that had invaded my bedroom. I never saw them alive. By the time I found them, they were already decomposing, hundreds of bees along the windowsill, piles dead on the floor. I have an elementary knowledge of physics, enough to understand if a butterfly flaps its wings in Belize it can cause a storm in Los Angeles, all things connected. As I stepped onto the coarse sand for the first time in Belize, is it possible the energy of my life changed, reverberated in a storm of bees in my bedroom countries away? The bees stained the curtains; they hung by their delicate wings, sticky from the brown sap of their bodies. The bees clung to the walls I'd painted the color of dried palm. Their thick dead smell stung my nose and eyes. Were the bees a signal—beware?

Even though I'm a woman who looks for signs, I sometimes ignore the ones I don't want to see. I swept up the tiny bodies and wings, scrubbed the walls and windows with an organic cleanser, and called an exterminator who wore a full protective suit and fumigated behind the wall with toxins.

I don't think about the bees as I sit on the beach with my feet in the Caribbean Sea. The sky hums, darkens, the wind hits my right side and trails across my body, my hair blows into my face no matter how I try to hold it back. I notice how quickly a storm enters the sky here, huge black clouds, plump like a belly, a womb not ready to release. The sea changes from teal to emerald, the waves bigger, capped in white. I don't know it yet, but the angry man is nearby under this same sky. Rage is building in him, dark like the turning clouds, sharp as a jaguar's teeth. In a few hours the angry man will unleash his violence on me. It doesn't occur to me to be afraid in this beautiful place, and if I sense a ripple of the angry man's life spiraling toward me out of control, I simply accept it as part of the natural landscape, wind and wave.

MYTH. The angry man slides his hand under a waitress's dress, feels her thick thigh, leans in to breathe her musk. She slaps him and he laughs. Earlier he sat in a room with his ex-wife and her parents, and no one spoke. At the end of the visit he smacked his wife's ass and left. He loves the smell of a woman. He loves the smell of a woman.

Under the blackening sky, I pray the same prayer I've been praying for months: for an experience of love so big I'll have to change my life to comprehend it. This is a new way of praying for me. I was raised on Catholic prayers, recited them like lists. When I was little, my favorite bedtime prayer was naming the apostles: Peter, Andrew, James, John, Philip, Bartholomew, Matthew, Thomas, James, Simon, Judas the brother of James, and Judas the Traitor. I zipped through the list every night, so proud to have come up with this prayer myself. As an adult, I drifted away from religion. I'm still not in sync with the Catholic Church, but in recent months I've been feeling pulled back and found a progressive church with a progressive priest I'm trying to learn from, not about ritual, but about a real relationship with love. This is new for me, too. Growing up, the nuns at school terrified me with the threat of God's love, how it could take me out of the blue the way it had taken them.

"I never thought I'd be a nun. Then one day, I got the calling. You have to be ready, girls. The calling could happen to you." For years I added to my nightly prayers: *Please God, please, please, don't make me get the calling.*

Now I pray for an experience of love so big I'll have to change my life to comprehend it. I mean romance. I mean with the diver. I ask love to break me open the way I expect the clouds to break open and pour out rain.

Tomorrow the diver plans to take me in a boat to his private caye, a tiny island along the coral reef. I think I'll snorkel off the edge of the sand and listen for the pirate ghosts he says haunt his island. Belize has a long history of pirates: Peter Wallace, Captain Henry Morgan, Blackbeard, and Jean Lafitte. Armed attackers still ransack tiny islands, so when the diver goes to his caye he shoots a gun at random intervals to warn away the would-be pirates. This appeals to my imagination, and I let myself build it up, wanting and not wanting to feel scared.

I think the diver will return tonight from work and tell me more stories about the corals and sharks. His favorites are the whale sharks, the biggest and friendliest fish in the sea. They grow to sixty feet long and have three hundred rows of tiny teeth inside their cavernous mouths. They could swallow him whole yet if he forced his way through a whale shark's mouth, the shark would turn its stomach inside out to expel him. Instead, they feed on the tiniest plankton traveling the sea's currents. The diver wonders if whale sharks take advantage of their colossal size against the microscopic plankton, but he figures whatever created them must have designed them this way on purpose. He's dived with thousands of whale sharks and knows some of them personally by marks on their bodies, missing dorsal fins, propeller scars from big ships, and tags from researchers. I think he's like a whale shark, big and playful and gentle.

Imagine breathing underwater, the diver says. That's a lovely thing.

I never learned to scuba dive. I enjoy hearing about the world that exists below, but I have no desire to strap a tank on my back and dive deep. Even snorkeling gives me pause. I'm a strong swimmer and amazed by the corals, but it makes me uneasy to see all those fish up close, so many of them, and some are big, swimming right next to me. I can't explain my resistance to fish, but I've had it all my life. My grandfather used to take me fishing, and I was always relieved when no fish bit my line. I didn't want to reel one in, touch it, and see it squirm on the hook. I don't even eat fish or seafood—the taste, the texture, the smell—no, not for me. I have a private theory that I'm deathly allergic to some type of fish so my body revolts at the mere thought of consuming any. Even so, it's an awkward theory when I'm dating a man of the sea who lives in a Central American village along the Caribbean coast. I don't admit this to the diver, but I prefer to swim oblivious to whatever I'm joining in the sea.

Diving is not something anybody should be forced to do, the diver says. It should be something you want to do. You should do it because you feel the urge.

MYTH. The angry man's mother was from a border town. His father was a Guatemalan cowboy. His abuela washed clothes against a stone in the lake. When he was a child, he helped her some Sundays when most of the other women attended church and the men played soccer. He wanted Abu to himself. He wanted to grow up and escape.

MYTH. The angry man wears a jaguar tooth necklace so that some of the jaguar's power will rest on his chest, as if the energy of the animal can be transferred, like heat to cold.

FACT. This is how heat travels. Warm molecules move faster than cool molecules. Put a warm object on a cool object, and the fast-moving molecules collide with the slow-moving ones, giving up some of their heat to warm the cooler thing.

On the morning of the angry man, I sit on a breathtaking beach while the diver leads a group of tourists underwater. I think I'll wear my black sundress with pink trim tonight. I think I'll sit at dinner and tell the diver stories about my life in Los Angeles. The diver likes hearing about the house I recently bought and started renovating. I think I'll tell him how I keep catching the neighborhood kids peeking into my windows while I'm sanding the wood floors. I've been winning the kids over by giving them art supplies to use in the driveway and whispering to the two main culprits that I have a very important job for them: They're in charge of making sure no one ever, do they understand, never, peeks into my house. Can they handle the job? Yes, yes, they agree, they're in charge! I think the diver will smile his sweet smile. I think we'll walk together along the beach. I think I'll ask the diver about the strange seaweed that reaches out from the water and strangles my feet.

He'll return tonight, but by the time I see him again: X.

X will mean many things.

X will shift with the shifting tides of the angry man and me.

X will take that horrible turn down the dark dirt road in Maya Beach, and the whole of everything after that will change.

The angry man is somewhere nearby gaining strength and speed, taking on the wild nature of a beast. Soon he will hit me with his full force and break me apart, spin me into a different orbit—parts of me will fall, bit by bit, like broken light tumbling through clouds. Salt burns my chapped lips, but I lick it away unbothered. The palm trees weep, but I can't hear them. The trees know what is going to happen, and they are bending toward me in sorrow and anticipation. Beside me, the palm trees throw shadows on the sand. Their tears, mixed with the sea's unhurried salt, fall softly on the chain of events that's already in motion, nothing to stop what's coming.

FACT. Adult jaguars are at the top of their food chain. Nothing preys on them in the wild. They're most active at dusk and dawn. Cubs are born blind. Young cats stay with their mothers up to two years. Afterward, they travel alone.

MYTH. The jaguar got its markings by making paw prints on its skin with the sludge of the earth.

MYTH. Jaguars hold up the sky.

MYTH. The rosettes on a jaguar's pelt mirror the heavens—rosettes like blooms or broken rings of clouds around stars' dark eyes. The

skin of el jaguar is a blooming sky. The skin is blooming. The skin
is the sky, el jaguar, el jaguar.

●●

TWO

MYTH. The angry man kicks a grave in the jaguar sanctuary floor, big enough. It's an early hour when jaguars could be out—there's only a one-in-seventeen thousand chance he'll see one—but he keeps a sharp eye for Balam. The man is slow fury as he pushes his things into the handmade pit. First the red woven pouch he stole from the wrinkled Guatemalan lady whose name he can't remember, memories like money rush out of his life, water at low tide, the pouch empty too long.

He hears frogs from a creek in the sanctuary forest. The frogs make a tremendous noise. He brought his son once to hear these frogs. His son imitated the noise, and the angry man and his son laughed—papa's big boy—a laugh he hasn't heard since his boy was taken from home, the government on the angry man's back. He adds his bandana and T-shirt, drops them in the shallow grave. He is furious with despair in the summer heat. It's rainy season, more than 60 inches of rain from June to November, sometimes 160. It's

13

sure to rain today, his body can feel the steam, the rain before it falls. He lays out everything else he brought: a knife, a lighter, the joint he's about to smoke, a six-pack of Belikin beer, and a rope.

Balam. Jaguar. The ancient Maya worshipped the animal. Their kings were reincarnated as jaguars, and their shamans could transform into the animal, six feet tail to nose, 200 pounds, muscles that run. The angry man is part Maya, part Spanish, part animal, part man, part of his mind, part beyond reason. If he could be anything he'd be Balam—beautiful, rare, worthy of reverence and fear. Desperate, the angry man puts his foot on the rope.

FACT. The jaguar is the third largest cat in the world. The tiger and lion are bigger, but they don't live in this tropical forest, only the jaguar, along with puma, margay, jaguarundi, and ocelot. Jaguars sometimes use the trails to cross the sanctuary, leaving tracks and scat.

The angry man knows how to spot their tracks, he knows the forest, he's seen jaguars before, his eyes adjust to them, like elders who see spirits, going beyond sight to see animal mists in the dense green sea.

Balam will appear. The angry man can sense the animal in the basin.

I'm preparing for you, he says. He lets the wind carry the message to Balam.

The angry man sits beneath the tree with his feet in the grave, holds the knife in his right hand, and uncoils the rope with his left. He touches the knife to the rope, like the priest blessing his shoulder when he was a boy, then slides it against the rope lengthwise, as if to sharpen the blade.

He leans back on the thick root of the tree, sticks the tip of his knife in a crack in the root, opens a Belikin, and drinks the lager in several swallows without quenching his thirst. He knows if he harms the forest bad things will happen to him in life and after death; it's natural law.

Howler monkeys toss nuts from above. The frogs thunder. He finishes the second beer more slowly, tastes it in his throat. The third one is like water, easy, it goes directly to the edge of his rage and dulls it. He squints at the light trying to break through the canopy's massive ferns and palms. There are powerful things in the forest only wise elders and gods understand. The fourth beer builds his rage back up. He lights the fat joint, inhales deeply, holds the smoke in his mouth. He smokes and drinks until his plan makes sense again.

No more beer, the joint down to a blunt, his mind and heart in sync with disappointment and blame. His ex-wife, the government on his back. They took away his son. If there were a way to capture his boy and cross the Guatemala border he'd do it. His son is his life. They took away his life. The $10,000 fine he was slapped with for holding a joint might as well be $10 million. He won't go to jail, can't. He won't live without his son. He pulls the knife out of the root then plunges the knife in and out of the curve, the foot of the tree, its hard bones.

The canopy shines and shimmers dark to light to dark, plays with his moods. The angry man stumbles to his feet, circles the rope, kicks the empty beer bottles to the grave, and tosses in the lighter. He pulls the knife from the root and stabs the trunk of the tree once, a swift stab to the heart. He leaves the knife there, blade in the meat. He pisses on the side of the tree.

On other visits here, the angry man watched shy heron on the bank of the creek. He drank from the creek and never got sick, his stomach like a riverbed. Snakes, birds, butterflies, and lizards are in the trees and on the ground. The tropical forest is alive, but today he only looks for Balam.

FACT. There are hundreds of species of birds in the basin. Scarlet macaw, king vulture, bat falcon. When the sun blazes the birds rest in the canopy's shade, tucked among thick layers of leaves.

Carrying the rope, the angry man climbs, branch by branch, up the tree until he is high enough. He stabilizes himself and the rough bark bites his bare skin. He ties one end of the rope around a branch, and tugs at it several times to make sure it holds secure. He wants a beer or another joint or a woman to calm him down, anything to distract himself from how the vibration of the frogs' call carries the thought, again and again, of his son.

The angry man looks for Balam, but his perception is blurred like his thoughts, and he can't focus past the trees. To see Balam, he has to penetrate behind and between the trees, above and below, through the past and into the future.

The angry man loops the free end of the rope around his neck and ties a noose. He positions himself, feet on the branch, knees by his ears, crouches like a two-legged creature about to take flight, wet with sweat and fear. He looks at the green around him, so much green, rolling walls of green and a hard green ceiling and floor.

Come out, he says to Balam, I'm ready to die.

He isn't a man of hope. The regret of his life is constant. His knees ache in this contorted position. He runs his hand over his long hair, wipes it out of his face, and wishes he wore his bandana. He needs to see Balam before he jumps, hangs himself on the tree. Balam will give him final courage.

FACT. Jaguars are masters of stealth. They observe but are seldom observed.

The angry man senses Balam is watching him and peers down at the grave. Beside it, fresh jaguar prints, the size of a man's palm. He is locked in his five senses, can't get past them to find Balam, but he knows once he jumps Balam will eat his meat and leave his bones for the grave.

He spits at the belongings he left in the dirt. Spits at life. Spits at his ex-wife. At the government on his back. At his son. Spits like rain. Spits and curses Balam until he chokes and has to slide a finger between his neck and the noose.

The angry man crouches on the branch until his legs numb. He shivers with exhaustion. He is dizzy from holding his pose, and for a moment his mind blanks. He closes his eyes and sees jaguars. He opens his eyes and sees jaguars. Jaguars and jaguar spirits, two thousand jaguars suddenly populate the forest. He sees them between the trees, past and future, six feet tail to nose, some running, some still, jaguars with cubs, females in heat, outlined in mist, killing prey, drinking at the creek. Jaguars dot the basin like the rosettes of their fur. Their power makes him powerful. Their intense animal scent becomes his own. He feels strength in his legs.

He moves with animal grace and without thought. By instinct he unties the rope from around the branch and climbs down the tree. Balam stands next to the grave. Locking his stare on Balam, the angry man pulls his knife from the trunk of the tree, slices the loop of the noose, and lets the rope drop from his neck and the knife drop in the grave.

I'm ready, Balam, he says.

Balam will give him a death more honorable than the tree, and he is grateful for this new plan. He steps toward Balam, can hear the mighty cat's breath. He closes his eyes and contracts his muscles, tightens his body for the attack. He is waiting and adrenaline, he is fear and sorrow, he is silence and fury, he wants to live and he wants to die.

Howler monkeys and frogs bellow. Balam, the jaguar king, stands at one side of the grave, the angry man stands at the other. His son had imitated a frog, his son had smiled; he loved his wife once; he wanted a life he could live. He opens his eyes, and Balam and every jaguar are gone.

FACT. Male jaguars are solitary, living and hunting in territories they aggressively defend.

The angry man revs, his blood like oil slicking an engine, revs so high his muscles collapse. He falls into Balam's tracks, his hands where Balam's paws had been, his feet in the grave. His cheek presses the soil floor.

He can't start over. He can't reclimb the tree or retie the rope. He can't call Balam. Balam betrayed him—like everyone he's known. Ants crawl over his arms, bite him with their scissor jaws, scorching pain. He wants a joint. He wants a woman. He wants to tear Balam's head from the wild cat's neck. He pushes himself up to get away from the ants. Standing in the grave, he has to choose his next move. He stands for a long time, until the wind shifts and the sky goes gray, then he pulls on his T-shirt, ties the bandana over his long hair, and tucks the empty red woven pouch into the waistband of his jeans. How is he going to get money? He can't go on like this. He uses his knife to shovel dirt over the bottles in the pit.

When he's finished the angry man slumps against the tree. He stares at the rope coiled like a snake that's too tired and sick of itself to move. He wants his energy back. He wants someone to kiss this fear and anger away.

The canopy and clouds work together to block all light. Rainy season, the sky crashes and clangs, rain falls violently and soaks him with his own failure. He is cold and moves through extremes. He needs relief. Beer gives him backbone and spit, but he needs fire. He needs the heat of a woman, the only thing that ever warms him up.

He wants a sweet lick on his neck, a private moment to entice these demons, these million-pound ghosts off his back. Tomorrow he'll deal with tomorrow. Tonight he needs hands, hair, thighs, and flesh.

●●●

THREE

After the heat of the day, after the sky clears and the afternoon sun is no longer scorching, I close my book, the one about the boy stranded in a lifeboat with a tiger. I read most of the afternoon, longer than I intended. I felt compelled to continue reading, even though I kept telling myself to put the book down. I only brought one novel and wanted to savor it, little bits each day, but I read as if I were hungry for what it could feed me, until finally the boy in the lifeboat had a change of heart about the tiger. Then I breathed deeply and felt I could stop.

My body is stiff from sitting, I think a walk will feel good, so I tuck the book into the suitcase in my cabana, put a T-shirt and shorts over my bikini, and position my straw cowboy hat over my hair in a barrette, cooler that way in the heat. I toss some things in a backpack, I like to be prepared: camera, sunscreen, a twenty-dollar bill, twelve Belizean dollars, and a fifty-dollar traveler's cheque, just in case. I set off down the beach. When the beach gets swept up in waves,

I move to the road. A few cars pass but not many. This is a sleepy village, people don't go places just to go, why expend unnecessary energy?

MYTH. The angry man gets high on the beach under a coconut palm. He draws circles inside circles inside circles with a stick.

I walk and walk. It's farther than I remember. I'm going to the dive shop where the diver works even though he told me not to walk that far. I did it before, on my first trip to Belize, and he brought me back to town in a boat through the lagoon, naming vegetation and birds along the way. Red mangrove, black mangrove, buttonwood, heron, hummingbird, pelican, swallow, osprey.

As I walk I think about the marathon I recently ran, 26.2 miles, and how distance feels good to my body. But I'm in flip-flops, the wrong shoes for this road, and need more cushion against the small stones. The sandal thong rubs between my right toes and hurts. When I arrive at the dive shop, I plan to ask for a Band-Aid.

Along the road are brightly painted beach cabanas amid tropical overgrowth, and I think about the house I'm renovating. I call it a small bungalow because it sounds charming, but really it's a dump in need of total repair. It's toward the top of an uphill dead-end alley, which is misleadingly named a terrace.

The renovations have been harder than I imagined they'd be, and less fun. I watched my dad renovate an enormous house by himself. My brother renovated his home. My sister renovated hers; she even helped build a restaurant. The difference is they have skills

and power tools and like this sort of thing. I don't. I hired people
to take care of the big jobs: new foundation, plumbing, electrical,
and roof. But on my teacher's salary I don't have a budget to hire
professionals for all the cosmetic needs inside the house, so these
are my projects, and I have to do them on the cheap.

The biggest problem is the wood floors, which are uneven and
in horrible shape. I started with the easiest room, the bedroom,
which needed a few nails removed, sanding, and a new stain. Then I
moved to the living room and kitchen floors, which were burdened
by a layer of carpet and underneath that a layer of linoleum that was
glued to the wood. I pulled up the worn-out carpet and dragged
it to the driveway. The driveway is being supported by hard dirt
packed around an overturned porcelain claw foot tub; the house
inspector had never seen anything like it, but laughingly told me
it was the least of my problems. On the floor, I used a little metal
tool to scrape up the linoleum and moved around the room on my
hands and knees testing for weak patches that would come up easily.
Soon the floor resembled a map of gluey continents, shifting plate
tectonics, and then not only were the floors structurally uneven,
they were sharp and sticky to walk on, too. It was so much worse
than when I started.

Employees at the late-night mega-hardware store in Hollywood
sold me tools and various liquids and goo in large containers. I
tried their suggestions, took photos of the disastrous results, and
returned to the store where invariably different people would
be working so I'd whip out the series of photos and explain the
project from the beginning, asking, What do I do now?

When I finally admitted defeat with the floors in these rooms, I called in an expert who assessed the mess and shook his head. The wood floors were never worth saving to begin with, he said, they're soft wood, not hard, and no way was I going to get up those tiles, better to start over. I forked over the money for him to lay plywood over the current floors in the living room and kitchen as a base for new hardwood floors. It's a great idea, but hardwood is expensive and will have to wait. What do I do now? Paint, trick the eye with color! After days of indecision, I settled on dark orange for the floor. Yes, orange. I was inspired by a book of dream homes in Mexico, and I decided those colors are my palette. I painted the plywood dark orange and finished it with a sealer. The baseboards were gone, oh well, one more thing for the list. I painted a faux finish on the walls in yellow and orange. Then I went all out and laid huge purple tiles on the plywood in the kitchen. I quickly discovered I'm not a good measurer. I'm an approximator, which isn't the best quality to have for home renovation. The tiles approximately meet with the edges of the room. It will be covered once the baseboards are up, but what do I do now? Hide some of the gaps with floor plants! If I don't look too closely at the unevenness—and the fact that the floor is plywood and that there are no baseboards—and just take in the gorgeous plants against the wild color scheme, the house is starting to look festive, if not beautiful.

As I continue to walk along the road past a pink house with green trim, an orange and blue house, and one painted yellow and red, I make mental notes while the camera in my backpack bangs against my spine. I wonder if I could afford to buy a tiny house here and if I could make it home.

I'm thirsty. I have money, but there's nowhere to buy water. The road to the dive shop stretches out longer and farther. I don't know what time it is, but the air is cooling. I hurry. I consider maybe I should have listened when the diver told me not to walk. I want to spend every minute of the rest of this day with him but when I get to the dive shop I'm surprised it's already closing. He left work an hour ago to be with me. He must have gone home on the water while I was on the road. My heart sinks, and I feel foolish. My cell phone doesn't work in Belize so I call him from the dive shop office and tell him where I am. I laugh at the situation and apologize for not being at the cabana. I tell him I'll catch a taxi and meet him in a few minutes. He says he'll wait in the hammock on the cabana porch. He says he misses me.

MYTH. The angry man's father had a reputation for drinking. The angry man watched his mother take the brunt of it.

The dive shop doesn't have a taxi phone number so I go to the restaurant next door, and the bartender makes a call. I step to the road to wait for the taxi. I could stand outside the dive shop or the restaurant where there are other people mingling, but the buildings are set back from the road on a small cul-de-sac, and I don't want to waste a moment returning to the diver. I want it to be easy to jump in the taxi and go. I remember the O. Henry story of the couple that had no money for Christmas presents. He sold his cherished pocket watch to buy her hair combs. She cut and sold her hair to buy him a chain for his watch. I think the diver and I are a little like that couple. He left early on the water to be with me while I was traveling the road to be with him. I think I'll tell him the story when I see him. I think he'll kiss me for that story.

You have to learn to breathe from a regulator, the diver says. When you're underwater you inhale and exhale through your mouth. Your nose is inside a mask so if you exhale through your nose you might create air space, which will cause the mask to fog up or allow water to clear. Then your view will be less.

I'm impatient, where is the taxi? Each car that passes makes my heart jump in anticipation. Finally a reddish orange van comes down the road. The driver, a striking guy in his thirties, about my own age, stops.

Taxi! he says.

It doesn't look like a taxi and there's a younger man in the front seat, but taxis here come in all colors, makes and models, and friends or family members often go along for the ride. I don't notice many of the details of this taxi. My mind is preoccupied with the diver. I respond yes! The passenger jumps out and walks quickly up the road, turning once to give me a piercing or maybe encouraging look; I don't know how to interpret it. Later, on another day, I will wonder about that guy in the passenger seat. Did he suspect what was going to happen? Did he try to send a message with his eyes? Or was it nothing, just a look? I hop in the front seat of the taxi, which is customary. The driver pulls a U-turn and heads toward town.

MYTH. The angry man's mother loved to waltz. When he was very small, she used to dance him through the narrow space between the wall and the couch. He was proud to waltz with his mother, especially since his father had no rhythm. Then the angry man's mother waltzed alone, while her boy and his father watched.

●●●●

FOUR

I sit with my backpack on my lap chatting with the taxi driver. He has a distinct Mestizo look, seems out of place in this Creole village, an artist, I think, on the fringe. He reminds me of friends at home. I like the way he tied his red bandana over his long hair, notice the remains of red fingernail polish on his left thumb, and wonder why he painted his nails and if he has a thing for the color red. Maybe he's a painter or a musician. Maybe he plays music on the beach—wine flowing, good food, a bonfire. I've never seen anything like that in the village, but maybe it's because I hadn't met him yet and didn't know where they gathered. I wonder if the diver knows him though I doubt they'd have much in common.

Underwater there are signs you use to communicate, the diver says. Okay. Up. Down. Slow down. Something's wrong. Low on air. Out of air. Watch out for that big fucking shark!

He seems like a friendly driver, and I hope for an interesting conversation, but I'm confused that he doesn't recognize the name of my hotel in this tiny village. It's one of the most popular places to stay. There are nearly a dozen cabanas on the property, which is located at the very end of the road, any farther I'd be in the bay. *Why doesn't he know?* He mentions he was watching the soccer game with the guy who was riding with him, and the local team won. I'm glad because I know this will make the diver happy. I guess that the taxi driver's been drinking and carefully explain where I'm going, using local references which gives me a slight twinge of pride to be in-the-know.

I ask how much the fare is. He says BZ$20, but he'll give me the ride for BZ$15 since . . . I can't hear his reason or maybe he mumbles or maybe he doesn't finish his sentence. *Great,* I think, *a discount.* I ask if he has change for $20 US, and he doesn't. Again, I find it strange for a taxi driver not to have change, but it's Sunday and things in this village are relaxed so I'm not concerned. I check my backpack and tell him I can either give him BZ$12 or I need to stop somewhere for change. It's up to him. He says he'll stop.

MYTH. When the angry man was still young, his father died and his abuela grieved. After the priest gave the last anointing and said, "Amen," after Abu covered her dead son's face with the small blanket she had stitched so many years ago for his baptism, after she cried in private because he had never been a good boy or a good man, she took her grandson's hand and led him to the trailhead. They walked the easy loop, careful of the sharp sprouts and with an eye out for animal tracks. They stopped to watch a

Blue Morpho drink from rich mud and flit around the branches of a rotting log. As the butterfly flapped its wings, it seemed to appear then disappear, blue then brown, blue then brown, here then gone, son then no son, father then no father.

Abu told him be still. He held his breath and froze.

I can feel your papa inside the butterfly, she told him.

Then with the magic of a grandmother, Abu suddenly caught the butterfly in her cupped hands.

I think he's apologizing, she told him.

To you?

Yes. And you.

She handed him the butterfly. He took it in his little boy fingers, studied its blue side, brown side, body, and legs. Then he plucked off one of the wings. Abu snatched the butterfly, pried open the boy's mouth, and crushed the butterfly inside. He gagged, spit out mangled pieces, slapped at his tongue with his hands, then sat on the trail, crying.

Get up, she told him.

It took him a long time, but she waited. Then Abu placed an open palm on the top of his head, bent down, and kissed both his eyes.

You're like your father, she told him.

No I'm not.

I love you, but you are.

FACT. Blue Morphos aren't really blue. They have tiny scales on their wings that reflect blue light, making them appear to be one thing when they're really another.

We drive halfway to town. I'm struck by how far I walked. I hold my backpack on my lap, anxious to get to the cabana and hop right out. I'm annoyed it will take longer since we have to stop somewhere for change. He suddenly pulls left off the road onto a path in the sand that leads to two houses facing the sea. He says he'll stop at home for some money so he can give me change. He turns off the van, gets out, comes around to my side, and opens the door. I get a strange feeling. He says there's a restaurant up the road, and he'll go there for change. Now I'm nervous, he just said he was going home, why the discrepancy? I want to get out of the van, but he blocks my way. He reaches across me for his red woven pouch from the console of the van. I don't like his body pressing against mine, and I clutch the backpack to my chest. He slowly moves the red pouch and in a split second, before I can see what's happening, he holds a knife to my chin and pins my arms with his other hand. I gasp, pull back from him, try to burrow my body into the seat. My heart slams against my chest, his mouth next to mine, his breath hits my lips, I taste metal.

Don't do anything stupid, he says. I'm not a regular taxi driver.

This is what he says. I'm not a regular taxi driver.

He says, I'm going to rob you. I want all your money. Do what I say.

He says it this way, like he rehearsed it, like lines from dialogue written on paper. It seems forced. He forces himself on me, body and knife.

He forces himself on me, body and knife.

I shove my backpack toward him.

Here, take everything, I say. Don't hurt me. You can have everything, I have a good camera, it's worth a lot of money, here.

I'm not going to hurt you, he tells me, pressing the knife to my jaw. I don't want your camera. I want your money. I have to get home.

Please don't hurt me.

I'm not going to hurt you. Just do what I say.

He closes the door of the van, and I hear a click from the outside. Click. A key turning? The door locking? A latch catching? Click. If there is one dominant sound I will always associate with the angry man, it's that click. Years from now I will still be able to hear it in my right ear, always the right, never the left, memories find tiny rooms in the body to live. Sitting in the van, I'm paralyzed with fear. I don't even consider moving, let alone fighting. My mind races. *What was that click? Does the door open from the inside? Am I trapped? Why didn't he take my money?*

FIVE

The story of X isn't about X. It is but it isn't. Stories are written or lived or told, and they turn out to be different than what they seem to be. The taxi driver isn't a taxi driver. He's in a costume that zips up the back. He's an imposter, a concoction, a jaguar in a man's clothes. He has a heart made of mud.

He returns to the driver's seat, says he's from another place. He's not a taxi driver. He's an outlaw. He's on the run. He stole the van and needs money to get home. He tells me this as he closes his door, both of us now in the cage. I can see the landscape without turning my head, sand and water, a house far off. The sun is setting in magnificent streaks of pink on top of blue, sliding quickly down the sheet of sky, bouncing on the edge of earth before it finally drops into its dark, silent well.

The angry man's eyes turn dark along with the sky, and his anger emerges, a storm with no rain touching ground. The angry man reaches across my lap. Hand becomes knife. He holds my arms against my body, and the knife on my side. A surge of electricity races through me, every cell on fire. I don't scream—even if there were someone to hear it my throat can't make the sound.

It's hard to breathe. I suck shallow air and tell him again, Take everything I have, just don't hurt me.

He says, I'm not going to hurt you, don't do anything stupid, shut up, what do you have? He insists he doesn't want my camera, just needs money. $20 US and BZ$12? He's furious that's all I have.

He needs more, he needs to get home, the government fucked up his life, they took his son. His breath is the smell of stale alcohol in my face. He's high and desperate and his own adrenaline pushes him past frenzy.

The angry man turns on the ignition, reverses the van out of the sand back to the road and careens away from town. *He's going the wrong direction. Where is he taking me?* He holds the knife with his right hand and drives with his left. His arm and the knife hold me in my seat.

Never go diving without a plan, the diver says. Plan your dive and dive your plan. In a situation where you're scared, it's very important that you stop, think, and then act. Stop, think, act.

Things change. They're not what they appear. Taxi driver becomes abductor. Paradise becomes nightmare. Fear, like poison, burns through my veins. Fear wraps around me and shrinks me into a new shape. What am I? A grasshopper. I try to camouflage myself on the seat. I lack armor. I'm a little insect holding the backpack to my chest as if it can shield my smallness. I want to jump under the dashboard or hide in the crack of the seat until I can slowly inch along the door to find a way out through a hole in the rusted metal. Fight or flight? Neither is an option. I tell myself I'll be okay. *I'll be okay. I'll be okay. I'll be okay. What's the signal for okay?*

TRUTH. I'll be okay.

TRUTH. I am okay.

TRUTH. There's never a time I'm not okay. (Define *okay*.)

MYTH. Balam appears on the road in front of the van. The angry man has his hands full with the tourist, or he'd stop the van and fuck up the cat. Balam deserves an ugly death for the way it betrayed him in the forest. In a flash the angry man sees himself driving Balam instead of the tourist. He presses the knife to the tourist's chest. He imagines turning the blade, stabbing Balam in the heart. The cat collapses, lays its head on the angry man's lap, makes a dying guttural grunt. The angry man strokes the jaguar's cheek. Then he slides his hand under the deep fur of the jaguar's neck, reaches in, and pulls out Balam's final breath. Balam's teeth spill onto the floor of the van around the angry man's feet. The angry man scoops up a tooth in his fist and tells himself he's a man of power. A jaguar man. He sees himself seated on an ancient temple throne, a jaguar coat on his back and a jaguar head atop his head. As he races down the road in his van, gunning the accelerator, he's the conqueror of speed and might.

FACT. A jaguar's teeth are used for biting, scraping, cutting, and crushing. Its jaw is powerful enough to pierce a turtle's shell or pulverize bone.

The jaguar man tells me to take off my stupid hat. I do. My hands are shaking. He tells me to put my hands on my knees. I do. My terror convulses against my bones and skin, trying to find a way out. I hold my body as still as I can so he won't notice, but it's hard to keep from quaking. He says he's going to take me to Maya Beach where he will rob me and leave me there. He says it will take me a long time to get back, and he'll have a chance to get away. The knife is on my side. He's driving fast. He says something about turning over, something about how he'll take my money if we don't turn over. He asks if I know what he means? My voice trembles, yes, I understand what he means. He means he's driving very fast. It hadn't occurred to me that the van might turn over, but he thinks it might and now I think so, too.

I soothe myself the best I can—*I'll be okay, I'll be okay, I'll be okay*—but it's not working. The jaguar man is talking, what is he saying? I need to focus on him, but I can't listen to his ramble and soothe myself at the same time. *How am I going to get out of this? What is he going to do? What is he talking about?* My mind is rushing, my heart is pumping, the pressure on my internal levee is too great, my full fear explodes, the levee breaks, fear overwhelms me and floods my cells.

FACT. Physiologically speaking, adrenaline, noradrenaline, and cortisol rush through my bloodstream. (And his?) My nerve cells fire. (And his?) My system is out of balance. (And his?) Fire, increase, redirect, heighten. Fire, increase, redirect, heighten.

Click. Click. There's that sound again. Only these clicks are internal, and I literally feel them as physical sensation. Two clicks, one in my chest under my breastbone, then one in my gut. It's the same sound as the van door locking, but this door is in me. Click. Click. It startles me though I don't have time to ponder it now. Later I will realize the clicks were parts of me turning off, detaching.

The emotional body has its own way of taking care of itself. It's engineered to withstand mounting pressure but push it past its limit—there are limits—and its circuits short. Fear sets off an automatic lockdown. The body orchestrates a new order. Every thought and emotion that isn't absolutely necessary turns off, valves with no release. My fear never fully retreats, but the kind of terror that can get in the way of survival clicks, clicks down one notch, then two, until my teeth stop chattering and I go acutely still underneath my shaking body. I suddenly feel far away from myself, like I've been sucked through a vacuum hose.

Where does the terror go? It has to go somewhere. Mine is like a helium version of myself rising, rising on a Caribbean breeze until my hair gets caught in a tree and I'm stuck, overhead, watching my other part below, the part still listening to the jaguar man, the part still attached to the gristle and meat of my body. I become her, she, you. We're fuzzy, opaque, confused people split in parts, hovering above and in the van. Not exactly someone else, but I'm not me. Not here with a knife pressed into her belly. She's the balloon, or you're the balloon. I'm the meat or she or you.

FACT. Watching something happen changes the way it happens. The more you observe, the greater the effect.

Now you can think. Your mind clears. You are singularly focused, more so than any other time in your life. Your mind becomes a chasm so empty that any tiny dot of thought is impossible not to notice. This works in your favor. You're not distracted by the past or worried about the future. The only thoughts that enter your mind are ones that instruct you now.

Your first thought. *Cooperate, don't fight, don't resist.* Don't let the jaguar man stab you.

Second thought. You remember a friend back home who was stabbed multiple times, how his body blew up twice its normal size, how it took a team of emergency doctors in a trauma hospital to keep him alive, how there's no hospital here, no clinic, no nurse. You haven't seen a car or person for miles. If the jaguar man cuts you, you will die. Don't let him stab you. Do whatever it takes. *Do whatever it takes.*

Third thought. *Dear God, please let me live.*

You: Please don't hurt me.

He: I'm not going to hurt you.

You: Please don't hurt me.

He: I'm not going to hurt you.

That's your call and response. You say it every chance you get. You want his reassurance. You want him to say his part over and over, I'm not going to hurt you, say it until it's true. There's a knife on your side. He's not going to hurt you. Can both exist simultaneously?

Diving is like floating, the diver says. It's an underwater space walk, no gravity, up, down, sideways, backward, roll over. It's stress free, no effort. If it's done properly the current will take you, easy and relaxed.

Words shift. The story shifts. You're in the van with the jaguar man driving down an unlit road to God knows where. There are no people, no signs of life, no one to call for help. The diver is a world away. For a split second you see yourself unlocking the door and jumping out. The trees blur with the picture in your mind. His knife presses hard against your stomach, the knife tells you stay where you are, don't move.

You can master staying in one place without moving up or down, the diver says. You can stay neutral by controlling your breath.

You barely breathe. You keep your hands on your knees. Information comes to you in flashes. You know the jaguar man will X. In your mind you agree to let him.

In my mind I agree to let him?

In your mind you agree to let him.

A knife in the jungle contracts its own terms. Some terms don't make sense except in the moment. For you, there's no questioning or angst, it's not even a decision. It's a split-second deep knowing: the jaguar man will X. X is not your life. X is the high holy offering you will make, the sacrificial goat with a flower in its mouth you will place at the jaguar man's feet so he will decree that you live. This is a steep price, but you're willing to exchange this for that. You give, you get. You tell yourself you'll cope with X later, God willing, just don't let the knife penetrate your skin.

Is it X if you let him?

It is unequivocally X, even if you let him.

SIX

Belize, beautiful Belize. On your first trip to Belize, you felt lucky to be solitary, the only person on a beach, your very own sand, water, hammocks, chairs. You took an embarrassing number of photographs of empty hardwood beach chairs, the sturdy kind that withstand constant exposure to the elements, slough off salt, rain, and the blistering sun. You called the photos your empty chair series. Your friends were annoyed. They wanted to see action shots of your excursions snorkeling and caving.

What do you mean you don't have pictures of the diver?

Photo after photo you showed them chairs. Pink chairs, blue, green, yellow, orange, newly painted, faded and chipped, scratched and worn, so many empty chairs, most of them low to the ground, their seats hovering just over the sand, and a few tall barstools at the edge of the outdoor beach bar. Chairs the colors of the Caribbean, colors you could use in your house.

You didn't position the chairs. You photographed them as you found them.

See, this one is facing the sea. This one is touching another, arm to arm. This one has its back to the circle of others.

Where are the people? your friends wanted to know.

Who cares? It was your beach! So many chairs to choose from! You imagined returning to these chairs. You imagined how the diver and you would find two chairs facing the sea and listen to the waves play the washboard of sand, play and recede, play and recede, a private, old-time band.

Back in Los Angeles, you prayed your prayer: God, give me an experience of love so big I'll have to change my life to comprehend it.

MYTH. The jaguar man plunks his son on an outdoor barstool, orders a beer for himself and Coke for the boy. He scans the place, eyes a firm ass on a woman he doesn't recognize. He's trying to be good, win back his ex-wife. He's sorry for his mistakes, he'll change, she'll forgive him if he can stay out of trouble. (His boy taps his arm, says Papa.) Plus he's got the kid with him. But damn, he can't help admiring that ass.

SEVEN

The jaguar man turns off the road onto a side road then takes a
dirt path off that. The dirt path has a cluster of downed trees in
front of it acting as a blockade. This path leads toward the sea. You
wonder if the trees fell or if they were put there to keep people
from driving down the path. He maneuvers the van around the log
barricade, pulls the van into the thick tangle of tropical overgrowth,
then backs out and reverses it so the van is facing toward the path.
You think this is for an easier get-away. *Is it possible he's been here
before? With other women? What is his plan?*

He stops the engine, silence all around you.

Maybe he's thinking about his next move, but you don't
anticipate anything past this moment. Maybe he's aware of the
movements of the forest, but your focus is intently on him.

The detached part of yourself is hovering above, holding the
helium of your fear. Your body is in the van. One day you will reach
back in your memory to when you were sitting in this van and

you will be unsure how to describe it. You will remember specks of detail: a radio knob, a split seat, a cracked windshield, but even these memories will have question marks behind them. Memories are tired tricksters. They have to unwrap themselves, say drawn out goodbyes to their hiding places, and carve their own long, circuitous routes over an endless option of pathways to the mind. By the time they reach a place where you can grab them, who knows how much they've changed.

FACT. The van was parked in the jungle beside the sea.
FACT. The van was red or orange.
FACT. The van was a van or an SUV.
FACT. It had a backseat.
FACT. It had windows that were hard to see out of or it was dark or you didn't turn your head.
FACT. The jaguar man sat beside you. You didn't move until he told you to. But that doesn't describe the van.

Try. If it had a smell it would be dark. The van would smell torn up. It would smell busted and dirty. It would smell old and angry, like stale beer, weed, and sex. It would smell like a tight grip on a small arm. It would smell like fear, like night descending fast, a blanket thrown over the horizon. Or it could, you suppose, smell backward, like reaching back in time to another place, maybe childhood, playing outside, killing ants on ant piles, birthday parties, apples, drugstore perfume. More likely it would smell like the scent rising from the dusty dirt road, pocked with ruts and stones. If it had a smell, which it did (you just can't recall it), it would be tangy earth mixed with gasoline and seaweed. It would be the smell of a leak, a dial turned almost off, the fumes of yesterday's shit, the sickly-sweet smell of underarms and sweat, fish fried in oil, the smell of a shiver down someone's back, like another woman was trying to scream, was gurgling through the hose of her throat, seeing into her future, her head against the window, legs splayed on the seat.

The jaguar man says he's not a bad person.

You say you believe him.

Sitting beside him in the van, you can tell he's in pain, not physically but the deeper desperate suffering that drives people to madness. His pain is palpable. His pain. *His, his.*

QUESTION. How did X become a women's issue?

He asks again how much money you have.

Wait. Go back. Let's be clear about X. You know it's coming, right? He's predictable, right? Like so many other sick men all over the world, right? X belongs to *him*. X belongs to his anger and madness and deficiency. It belongs to the muscles he's flexing to feel mighty. It belongs to his meagerness, fear, and confusion. It sits in the lap of his own self-loathing. It's not personal to you. You did nothing wrong. The jaguar man will press against you, force you to carry some of his pain (and it will affect you profoundly), but X is not your issue.

Here, put on a mirrored armor and deflect X back to its source.

You politely tell him the same as before. $20 US and BZ$12. You remember the $50 traveler's cheque and tell him he can have that, too. He gets out of the van and comes around to your side.

You hope once you give him the money he'll leave you here. You want him to leave but you're also scared to be left. You have no idea where you are or how to get back to the village.

He opens the door, tells you to take all your things. He's going to leave you. Then he asks if you can drive.

Yes, you can drive.

But first, the money. He stands over you, blocking the door, his knife pointing at you while you sit in the passenger seat and shuffle through your backpack to find your money. You can't find your money pouch. You're desperately looking, panic growing. He gets fed up and turns on a light, a flashlight or the van light, you don't know which, but there is light. Your pouch is sitting beside you on the seat. You take out all the money and the traveler's cheque. You get a pen, you don't know if it's yours or his, but suddenly you're holding a pen, and you sign the cheque. He tells you to put your passport number on it. You don't know your number so you make up one. You write it on the front under your signature.

It goes on the back not the front, he growls. What are you trying to pull?

You rewrite your passport number on the back. You have to keep flipping the cheque over to duplicate the number you wrote on the front. You explain you're just nervous, but he's suspicious. He looks at your signature. Your hand was shaking so violently your signature is illegible, and he thinks you're trying to trick him. He's furious.

Are you trying to make your signature not match? It's more accusation than question. He grabs the cheque and crumbles it.

Forget the damn cheque. Get out.

EIGHT

FACT. Jaguars travel along roads, on paths and trails in the forest, beside streams and creeks. Though they traverse with a light touch when hunting, other times jaguars make deep scrapes in the dirt and on trees, markings that signal where they've been.

SOUVENIR SNAPSHOT. Jaguar crossing a road.
SOUVENIR SNAPSHOT. Jaguar astride a tree branch.
SOUVENIR SNAPSHOT. Jaguar in a full-throated roar.

MYTH. Yesterday the jaguar man crept around the back of his ex-wife's house. He crouched low, flattened a bed of tall grass, and waited to catch a sign of his son. His ex-wife may have tossed him out like dirty water, but she has no right to keep him from his boy. He planned to grab the boy, sneak off with him through the green darkness to the Maya ruins, and sit his son on the Jaguar Temple so his son could be initiated into the legacy of his people. His ex-wife didn't bother with these things, and she can't teach the boy to be a man. The jaguar man waited in the grass, long after his boy went to bed, until he saw his ex-wife cross in front of a window. She seemed to taunt him, the way she walked across the room, but he could tell there was no other man there, so he left.

SOUVENIR SNAPSHOT. Jaguar chasing a boar through the temple plaza.

You stand beside the van, surrounded by night. Even the moon behind steel-gray clouds seems to have spun away from you. The jaguar man says he'll leave you here with the stolen van and let you be the hero for turning it in.

He says he's not a bad person.

You say you believe him.

He says he has to tie you up so he has a head start.

Then he says he won't leave the van. He's changed his mind. He says he'll leave you here, but you can't report him.

You say everything you can think of to reassure him. You won't report him. You promise. You have no one to tell. He gave you his word that he won't hurt you, you can see he's a man of his word, you can see he's a good person, you're true to your word, too. You won't tell anyone. You promise. You won't tell anyone. You promise. You won't.

Your grandmother flashes through your mind, how her antidote to anger is love, how when your grandfather's anger flared she put her hand on his arm and kissed his forehead.

FACT. Sap from a Poisonwood tree will cause a serious, painful rash. Relief comes from applying bark from a Gumbo Limbo tree, which grows near the Poisonwood. The root systems of the two trees nourish each other—the pain and the salve.

The jaguar man tells you to walk, through the palms and thorny vines. He follows you, his footprints overlapping yours. He holds the waistband of your shorts and the knife to your back. The only witnesses are the sea and sky. This isn't a place people go to rob you. You think about women who are found cut up in pieces beside riverbanks, in ditches, in jungles and forests, or left on the side of the road. Will that be you?

You think of your parents. You think of the diver. You think it will be a very, very long time before anyone finds you on this deserted stretch of beach.

You think about the little boy in the book you're reading who's stranded in a lifeboat with a tiger. You read this afternoon through the scene where the boy has a change of heart. The boy stops imagining the ways the tiger can hurt him and starts believing he will survive. You tell yourself you'll be okay.

I'll be okay.

If it's your first time, don't go deeper than 15 feet, the diver says. A couple times later go no deeper than 40 feet. By the time you're open water certified, 60 feet is your limit. If you become advanced certified, then you can go to 130 feet max. Most underwater life is in shallow areas so there's no need to go deep other than for ego and curiosity. Diving has limits. If you go beyond that, it's a risk.

You formulate a set of instructions. Some are the jaguar man's exact commands. Some you infer. Either way (for one, two, three hours, the tip of his six-inch silver blade constantly on your skin), what you're to do is clear:

Talk in soft tones.

Keep your hands visible.

Don't call him sir.

Don't use that psychology on him.

Don't forget his knife is in charge, and he's ready to attack.

Don't make a sudden move.

Don't make him do what he's thinking of doing. That's how he says it. *Don't make me do what I'm thinking of doing.*

The jaguar man tells you to sit on the ground. He says he's going to tie your hands but not your feet. *He doesn't have rope though, what is his plan?* He uses the knife to cut the leather strap off your straw hat. He tells you to take off your T-shirt. He uses the leather of your hat to tie your wrists then wraps the T-shirt around your wrists for reinforcement. He takes off the rest of your clothes so you'll have to run naked into the street. You let him do these things. You don't fight. He removes your clothes like you're a child getting ready for a bath. You lift one foot, then the other.

Please don't hurt me.

I'm not going to hurt you.

The moon and the clouds spin the way you spin. At times you're in pitch darkness. At times there's light. He demands you lie back so he can show you he's a man. This is the first X tonight. Your body lurches. The part of you floating above lurches. Dark then light then dark, the energy of your fear reverberates in the moon and splinters into a thousand eyes of fire. As he presses his muscles against yours, you're here and there. You and her. Far and near. One part of you watches. One part takes the hit. You look past him to the stars. The bright eyes of the sky watch you and the jaguar man in the tangle by the sea. It hurts to look back at stars, hurts to see anything beautiful.

Personally, the diver says, I've been to 260 feet on air, which is crazy because the oxygen becomes toxic at that depth. What you see is a lot of darkness. It's eerie, like someone will attack you from the dark. You're in territory where you don't belong.

It's loud in your ears. X becomes noise, a clarion sound turning around on itself, stumbling, dancing the way it chooses to dance until it's not X at all. It's a wild horn that takes a deep breath and grabs you like it's got you by the tail. Notes rise and fall, the horn is in charge, and you can't say no. You can't say no. The sharp chords, the knife on your belly, won't let you say no. You don't have a clue why this is happening or how you're going to get home. This is unknown territory, a commotion of highs and lows, total nonsense and bedrock truth.

You clench to hold your body together. He snarls at you to tell him it feels good. You say nothing.

He demands you tell him how big he is, how unbelievably big. You tell him he's big.

He kisses your breasts, plays the knife over them. He tells you to turn this way, turn that way. It's awkward with your hands tied, and you can't move freely, so he unties you.

Do you have a husband? he asks.

You say nothing.

In the periphery of your vision you see green. A wild of green. Forest green leaves, sea green water, moss green barks of trees, yellow green shimmery sand, greens without names they're so particular to themselves. The black green curves of striated roots seem to beat like a subterranean womb. All around you is a mash of sand, snakes, mosquitoes, night bird calls, rhythmic waves, grasshoppers, and tall billowy green grass defending itself with sharp edges. You can hear the cries of the ground's hard bones: skull, teeth, long bones, ribs.

Nothing seems to last long and nothing is over quickly. You have no sense of time. Time is the size of each moment.

He wants to hear how good it feels.

You tell him he's big.

He's angry you won't say it feels good, a lie you refuse.

MYTH. When he was a teenager, the jaguar man wanted to grow bigger. He stole money from Abu and bought a small vial from the bush doctor. He drank the medicine and stared at himself waiting for something to change.

SOUVENIR SNAPSHOT. A male jaguar behind a female as if ready to mount. His open jaw bites at her neck.

You can't feel his hands or the sand and branches under your neck and back, the vines like fistfuls of hair. You can't feel him pounding into you. You can't feel his mouth rub against the grain of your skin.

FACT. A jaguar's rough tongue can peel skin away from flesh and flesh off bone.

You feel the sensation of the knife at all times. You feel it because you have to know where it is, but the nerves that register pain have turned off to assist you.

TRUTH. The knife is the worst part of the night.

The knife is the worst part of the night.

For a moment when he forces you on top of him and slightly outstretches his arms, you think, *Grab the knife and plunge it into his throat.*

Another woman in this situation might do it, fight. Somehow take possession of the knife. At least accept the risk of trying. But you, the thought makes you weak not strong, a fragile leaf in his fist.

The thought makes me weak, not strong.

You don't realize it yet but you have a powerful secret weapon. You've been falling in love, your heart is wide open. Wide enough to fit the only two men you know in this country: the one waiting for you at the cabana and this one in front of you. Wide enough to fit your mother who you want to hear from you again. And suddenly for the boy in the lifeboat with the tiger. The boy survives because he believes he will survive. The boy turns his fear into strategy. You remember this from the chapters you read today. The boy stops willing the tiger to die and lives with the tiger, in spite of the tiger, because of the tiger.

You're in your own lifeboat (knife, power, anger, beast), the discordant notes of it crystal clear. You need the jaguar man to be okay.

I need the jaguar man to be okay.

You can't rely on simple definitions. You may have entered the jungle with easy labels stuck to your chests. Hello, my name is right. His name is wrong. My name is good. His name is bad. My name is you. His name is he. But now you and the jaguar man are in a mixed-up state of we. One can't be okay without the other. You must embrace the man, do what his pain is begging you to do, not only for your own survival, but also for his. This thought flashes through your mind as you drift over yourself, watching the hideous knife stroke your terrified breast.

You and the jaguar man, horrible as it is, are in it together.

It means X.

X means two strangers shouting for help in private ways.

You want X to be over but you don't want him to die. You want him to heal.

I want him to heal.

For a split second you see him, really see him, not as he is now, you see underneath the violence of his life all the way to the crux of his nature where he is what you are. *Where he is what I am.* It's a fleeting insight but it's enough to guide you. You see what he's desperately trying to see in himself: he's not a bad person.

This shot of compassion slides through your body on an invisible thread. You use it to untwist your animosity and take the next full breath, bolstering your strength.

Instinctively your prayer shifts from you to him. *God, please love this man so much right now that he softens enough to let me live. God, please love this man. Please, God, please. Love him. Please.*

Maybe there's a God who answers certain urgent prayers in bolts of lightning, burning bushes, or angels somersaulting in the air. But it seems more likely messengers deliver powerful love, and there are only two of you on this pitch-black remote stretch of beach. Him with the red bandana, the knife, the anger, and pain. And you. Only two of you on this thin strip of X between the road and the Caribbean Sea. The compassion, the unbearable love he needs right now, can only come through you. You are the only possibility of an answer to your own prayer. God, you, and the man in the mash-up at the edge of the sea where bramble attacks sand on one side and water caresses it from the other.

What category of love is this? It's not romantic or familial, not love for a friend; it's not even agape love for all beings. This love is particular to him, jaguar love, love of survival, love born in snarls, love with teeth.

God, love this man. Love him. Please.

You don't realize its full effect yet, but this moment's compassion changes you forever. While the jaguar man hammers at your flesh, your unthinkable love for him carves a gash much deeper in your core.

NINE

The first rule of scuba diving is never hold your breath, the diver says. Diving underwater is its own world with a different atmosphere every 33 feet. The farther down you go the greater the pressure squeezes against your body, like a balloon or a chicken egg. If you hold your breath your lungs won't equalize. They'll compress. Ascending is even more dangerous because if you hold your breath your lungs overexpand and burst.

The jaguar man tells you to wash in the sea. You think he's clever to wash away evidence. Maybe he's done this before. You step into the water. It doesn't feel warm or cold. It's not even wet. You walk forward until the water is waist-high. Then you turn to the jaguar man and say, Okay! Bye! Like you're dismissing him. *Why do you say this? It makes no sense. Where do you think you're going? Where do you think he's going?*

He's angry you said goodbye. He doesn't like your tone. He's in charge, not you. He wades into the water toward you slowly. Your fear comes to life, more than before. You think he'll drown you. You think he'll hold your head under until your body goes limp, then drag you back to shore or leave you to bloat in the water.

FACT. Jaguars are excellent swimmers and will leap into water to catch prey.

SOUVENIR SNAPSHOT. Jaguar emerging from the water with a lily on its head.

But he doesn't touch you. He washes himself as he watches you wash. When you're finished you both step back onto the sand. You put on your shorts and T-shirt and carry the rest.
He says he's not a bad person.
You say you believe him.
He guides you down the road, away from the van. He says he'll leave you at the far end of the road so it will take longer for you to get help. You feel a glimmer of hope. Maybe he'll leave now. Maybe he'll give you the van like he said he would. You walk on the dirt road, numb to the rocks and thorns under your feet.

When diving at night you can lose your bearings, the diver says. You can think you're closer (or farther) than you are.

The jaguar man is calmer and asks you questions, sizing you up, taking his time. Where do you live? How old are you? He's curious about you. *Is he figuring out if he can trust you? What to do with you now? Does he want to connect?*
What's your name? You tell him the truth. He's already seen your traveler's cheque, it doesn't make sense to lie. Like a bully

on a schoolyard, he makes a pun of your last name. Oh, so you're "nothin'." This angers you. Of all things, this. You lash out in defense of your name. No, not nothing. Not nothing.

Who's with you on vacation?

No one.

You're on vacation alone?

Yes.

Who do you know in Belize?

No one.

What are you going to do when you go home?

I don't know.

Who are you going to tell?

No one.

Who's with you at your cabana?

No one.

Are you going to call the police?

No.

Why not?

I gave you my word.

Who do you know in Belize?

No one.

What are you going to do when you go home?

I don't know.

Sit on your bed and cry?

I don't know.

Sit on your bed and cry?

Yes.

FACT. It's easy to predict the movement of one pendulum in motion. Add a second pendulum and their swings become dependent, chaotic. Even slight changes in one lead to inevitable changes in the other. You can guess what might happen but you cannot be exact.

He suddenly tires and slumps. He says he considered killing himself today. This gives you insight. His pain is that severe. He's at the end of hope. He says he feels better and X calmed him down. He knows it was a bad thing to do but he's not a bad person. He wants to do things differently, but everything keeps getting fucked up.

You say you're sorry.

He says don't pity him. He says he's forced to do this.

You say things can get better.

He tells you don't say what you can't prove.

You ask if he prays.

Your own relationship to prayer is tenuous and haphazard (usually reserved for desperate times and, lately, some kind of big love). You're not sure how prayer works but you don't believe there's a separate entity out there that answers pleas. You suspect more likely the energy of your focus draws things to you. So you don't know why you ask if he prays, it surprises you when you say it, and it's the wrong question. He hates religion, the rules, the preachers who pretend to care, they took his son, the preachers and the cops, they're all the same, a $10,000 fine for a joint, and now they took his son.

He asks if you know Psalm 121? No, you don't know it. 122? You don't know that one either. He can't remember the number of the

psalm, the famous one, the one a lot of people use for a baptism—
his son had that psalm.

You haven't memorized any psalms.

What kind of Christian doesn't know the Bible? he yells.

The jaguar man is furious you can't recite a psalm. He tries to
recall the words of his son's psalm but he can't find the line.

Later you will look up Psalm 121, New International Version.
I lift up my eyes to the mountains—
where does my help come from?
My help comes from the Lord,
the Maker of heaven and earth.

He will not let your foot slip—
he who watches over you will not slumber;
indeed, he who watches over Israel
will neither slumber nor sleep.

The Lord watches over you—
the Lord is your shade at your right hand;
the sun will not harm you by day,
nor the moon by night.

The Lord will keep you from all harm—
he will watch over your life;
the Lord will watch over your coming and going
both now and forevermore.

You listen to him rant. You give him time and space to talk. You
hold your backpack, hat, and bikini and listen to the man who

just X riff on the sadness of his life. Palm trees shake, frogs squeeze their lungs to sound their calls, and grasshoppers rub hind legs against wings. The jaguar man becomes part of the soundscape: a competition of grumbles, grunts, a static buzz, caws and creaks, the scrape of palm against palm, the whoosh of wind, and slap, slap of the sea. His knife keeps an unsteady beat in the air as he waves it in front of you, crushes rhythm.

He asks if you pray.

This morning's prayer, for an experience of love so big you'll have to change your life to comprehend it, flashes through your mind. You think of the diver and wonder where he is, but you don't have time to linger on the thought. The jaguar man is waiting for an answer.

You tell him yes.

You offer to pray for the jaguar man. This surprises you too. It's not a premeditated offer—nothing with the jaguar man is premeditated—you're living moment to moment. He tells you people pray for him all the time, and it doesn't make any difference, nothing helps. He stares at you.

Are you going to report me?

No.

He doesn't believe you. You tell him you know he's a good person, if he lets you go you won't report him.

Prove it, he says. You want to pray for me, go ahead, pray, not like the preachers have my whole life, make it real.

That's what he tells you. Make it real. He transfers the knife from his right hand to his left and extends his empty hand. He wants you to hold his hand. He actually wants you to hold his hand.

MYTH. Balam stretches inside the jaguar man, a second breath, out of sync with his own breathing.

TRUTH. The jaguar man can violate your body, but he cannot violate your core. You are who you are, who you are, who you are. He cannot touch you there.

You put your things on the ground. You shut your eyes to find power deep inside you. A surge of feeling expands your heart. He wanted to kill himself this morning. You don't wish that pain on anyone. Pain so great he can't contain it in his body, and he's thrusting it on you. You shift your feet so your weight is evenly balanced. You hold his hand and take a breath. You're not sure how to start the prayer. The trees and waves and the moon in a thousand pieces whisper, *Go on, if he cares about life, any life, his own life, maybe he'll care about yours.*

You let your compassion for this man fill you. Love gives you strength that mixes with your fear and what emerges is a power that enables you to see beyond your circumstance.

QUESTION. If you care for your enemy, is he still an enemy?

Dear God, you begin, but you don't hear the words you speak. Your prayer is outside words, outside your body. You can't feel your hand holding his. It's a long prayer. You respond to everything he's been ranting about. It's not fancy but it's genuine. You pray that he'll feel better. You pray that his life becomes manageable. You pray that he will experience love and forgiveness. You pray that his relationships improve with his son and ex-wife. You pray for his troubles with the government to end. You pray that he'll have the will and desire to live.

Amen.

Amen.

It works. He softens.

That was a nice prayer, he says.

FACT. At a certain speed and frequency, two individual waves that are moving along the same medium in opposites directions overlap and cancel each other out. They produce a standing wave with several still points.

Silence between you. Then anger.

Was that real? Was that from the heart or were you pretending?

It's from the heart, you say calmly, soothing his erratic heat.

That touched me, he says, simmering now. A lot of preachers have prayed over me. You're the first civilian. That touched me right here. He points to a place below his heart. It makes me want to vomit.

A purge, you think. *He wants to purge.*

He reaches out to feel your chest. Your heart beats in triple time. You think he'll be furious that your heart is racing, but he tells you his heart is beating like yours.

He considers driving you home.

You pick up your backpack, hat, and bikini.

He says you've shown him a good time and he doesn't want to leave you in this place where it's not safe.

TEN

Then the jaguar man's conscience kicks in. Fire of a two-headed dragon. He feels guilty. He shouldn't have brought you here. He shouldn't have X. He tells you he's not a bad person, he's an outlaw, the government makes him do bad things, he's pushed, he can't think of anything else to do. His conscience agitates him. In a split second he becomes enraged, his full body threatening yours, mouth open, teeth bared, a new wind strengthening his storm, pushing you backward down the road farther away from the van, the knife under your chin, anger recharging him. The night's strange music shifts, screeches, screams. He panics. He knows what he's done is wrong and he needs to get rid of this, of you. The knife on your throat is lengthwise and ready.

The knife on my throat is lengthwise and ready.

He turns his wrist, and the knife's sharp edge bears down.

You tell yourself to not get cut.

The knife is poised against your artery.

Do not get cut.

He hisses at you to convince him that you won't tell a soul. Swear you won't report me! Who do you know?

No one!

Convince me! he screams. If you report me I will track you down and kill you! I have ways to find you! Convince me!

Everything in your world is upside down and backward, and you've lost the ability to discern real from unreal. He tells you he will hunt you down and kill you with such force it locks in your mind as fact.

FACT. He will hunt you down and kill you.
(Fact? He will hunt you down and kill you?)

Over and over, he demands to know if you're going to report him.

No, no, no, no, no.

What you're saying isn't convincing him. Say something else. You get out the words you can, against the blade. You have nothing more to say, no other thoughts. You panic now, eye to eye with his panic.

He's slipping into a new level of violence. A horn is screaming. The man is screaming at you to convince him. Your fear is so big it's every fear you've ever felt screaming at you now. The jungle is thick, and his anger is a vine wrapping itself around you.

FACT. A snake vine can coil around a tree like an insistent noose and strangulate the tree. Sometimes the tree will reverse the effect, grow around the vine to suffocate it so the tree can live.

He wants to hurt you. He does but he doesn't. He does but he doesn't.

You don't have time to think. You don't have a mind. You only have room in your entire body for one word. God. This is your prayer. The most basic prayer ever prayed: God.

This prayer can't unfold. It's either answered now or never. From the distance, a bus appears. You think how odd that a bus is driving out of the sea. Odd but no more bizarre than the rest of this night. Two huge headlights streaming over the wicked night. No sound at all, just light. Not the single beam many people see at death's door. These lights are of the earth, they're real, one for you and one for him, and they're coming right at you. You're relieved. You think someone on the bus will save you.

The jaguar man is startled by the lights. They shine across you and break apart the moment. Darkness is overcome. He lowers the knife and pushes you backward toward the puny dark headlights of his stupid, little van. It gives you time to breathe, a silent rest between chords. *But where is the bus? What happened to the lights?* The lights have disappeared.

Later you will wonder about these lights. Later you will be confused how a bus could drive out of the sea. You will tell people about the bus, and they will analyze the lights from different perspectives, looking for logical explanations. A fishing boat or a . . . they don't know what, but not a bus.

The jaguar man doesn't want to hurt you now, as the lights disappear in the distance as quickly as they came. He wants to connect.

He asks if he can have you again, do you know what he means? He asks, but his knife against your chest reminds you there's only one answer. You tell him it's been a long night. This angers him.

What? he demands, his knife coming alive.

Okay, you say, in a soothing tone.

You say okay.

This is the second X.

X turns over and over on itself.

X becomes a jumble of letters, *a-e-p-r*, which turns to pear, which means feeding him the fruit, the touch, the calm he demands.

This is what you do to not get cut.

After, he doesn't know what to do next. He seems drained.

Souvenir Snapshot. A jaguar lies on his side, his cheek on the dirt. A female swats at him with her round paw.

He leans against the bumper of the van while you stand facing him. He takes a long look at you, as if for the first time. He threatens to take you with him for a few days—a vacation together—he likes your company. He thinks you're a nice person.

You tell him it's time to go home.

ELEVEN

For one hour, two hours, three hours at the edge of the sea, words shift. The story shifts. You shift forever. Your new reality is announced. You love this man you hate the best you can so he softens enough to let you live.

The horn of your life is spiraling in chaotic notes, against his, in counterpoint. He's been improvising all this time and so have you. Jazz is like that. X is like that. Takes you on a ride, both of you so far gone it's hard to know where you are, let alone how to get back. You're reaching for another tune, a second life that's just beyond X and his fucked-up rusted van. You want the comfort of something familiar, anything familiar, and then with startling breath he throws you a line you recognize from where you originally started. He asks if you have money in your cabana. Money. That's the thread. He's back to money. Maybe all he wants now is money.

Maybe all he wants now is money.

You answer him yes.

How much?

You tell the truth, $100 US in cash, more in traveler's cheques. You say he can have it all. You give him what's in your backpack. $20 US and BZ$12.

You sit in the passenger side of the van clutching your backpack. He slowly drives down the deserted road. You don't notice that your other part, the helium balloon of your emotions, is still not with you. You leave her in the jungle to fend for herself. She's so weak it's easy to leave her behind. You don't even turn your head to see if she's stumbling to catch up.

He drives and talks. Relentlessly talking. He remembers Psalm 121 and recites it, but it doesn't make sense the way he says it.

He asks if you want him to drop you off at the police station.

No.

Why not?

You gave him your word.

He tells you he trusts you not to report him. He says to prove it he'll tell you his name. He introduces himself, first and last names, but whatever names he gives you fall out of your memory within seconds, like water through rocks. You will often wonder if he told you the truth.

He asks what you do for a living.

You're a teacher.

He's chitchatting now, a cabdriver with his fare. You notice the irony as the van retraces its steps down deserted dirt roads, passing the place where he first picked you up, taking you all the way through the village to your cabana.

When you get to the end of the village road where the cabanas are clustered, he parks the van then walks you down the long, dark, stone path. Your cabana is orange with a green porch. You pass the pink one, the green one, a yellow, a blue. You consider screaming for help, but there are no screams in you. You consider running but where? You don't think about the horrible things he could do to you behind a locked door, you don't question why you're still following orders. You keep walking, push aside overgrown hibiscus, yellow trumpets, coconut palms, the jaguar man behind you, his hand on your back. You're not sure where the knife is, but it must be near.

There are two orange cabanas at the end of the path, and you concentrate on getting to yours. When you get to your cabana, with the door facing the sea, the diver is still waiting on the hammock. This shocks you. You don't know how to respond, you don't want to reignite the jaguar man, don't want the diver to get hurt. You're disoriented to see the diver and you don't want him involved so you pretend you don't know him, ask if he's hotel staff. The diver repeats your name several times, asks what's going on.

The jaguar man gives you a suspicious look, you can feel his energy rise. You try to downplay your acquaintance with the diver so the jaguar man won't catch on. At the same time, seeing the diver gives you courage. You can feel the ordeal is nearly over. The only thing left is money, and it will be over. It will be over. You're almost there.

You unlock the cabana door with your key, which you find in your backpack, and the jaguar man follows you inside. The diver stands on the porch.

The jaguar man says, That guy seems to know you pretty well.
You say, casually, Oh, everyone here is really friendly.

You hand the jaguar man all your money. He only takes the cash.
You say loudly, Thank you for the taxi ride, I'm sorry I didn't have
enough money to pay you.

Under his breath he demands you walk him back to the van.
You do.

You ignore the diver who calls your name as you walk past him,
trying to figure out what's happening. His first thought is you picked
up the man in a bar, and you're on a date. Later he will be furious
you didn't give him a signal. He will feel helpless. He's a professional
diver, he doesn't just dive for himself, he dives for everybody around
him. He's trained in rescue so if something goes wrong he's there to
help people survive. But if he intervenes he might get hurt. You just
want to get through this moment, this moment, this moment, play
out your role to the end, compliant and calm, do what the jaguar
man says, get to the finish.

When you reach the road, you're suddenly confident. You're
in charge. You create meaning. In your mixed-up state of mind
you think how lucky that he picked you, you who could handle
it, you who never screamed or cried or resisted, who didn't make
him stab you, who saved a different woman from X, saved yourself
from dying, saved him from being a murderer. How does a
murderer ever know what direction to take next in life? If he had
killed you he'd be lost. He'll probably still be lost, maybe you'll be
lost, too, but it could have been worse. Above you the stars flicker,
eyes burning in the sky. The air hums like bees.

You notice his van is a shade of red or orange with a white license plate. If you see the license plate number it doesn't register. You've convinced yourself you won't report him, and your mind won't collect evidence. Later when you're told cabs have green license plates you wonder how would tourists know?

You tell the jaguar man you'll shake his hand and then he has to leave. You shake his hand and wish him many blessings. That's what you say. You wish him many blessings.

I wish you many blessings.

Later you will wonder why you said this but standing beside the van you bless him for your life, for bringing you home. And home has a whole new meaning. Home is where safety is. Home is where the diver you've been trying to reach is waiting, has been waiting, the man who tonight will hold you and whisper to you in his soothing voice to sleep, sweetheart, sleep.

The wind shifts and palm trees ache, as you turn away from the van and walk until you reach a place on the path where you think the jaguar man can no longer see you. Then you run, you run for your life, past the hibiscus and coconut palms, past the pink and yellow cabanas, off the path across the sand to your cabana. *Which one is it?* You can't see, you don't know where you are anymore, the trees are crying, salt in the air, the moon is full, the moon has pieced itself together again, but there are splinters of you still far away, left in the jungle.

The diver appears in the light. You scream, your first scream all night. DON'T HURT ME.

It's me, he says. It's me.

Someone calls out from one of the cabanas, Are you alright?

You don't answer, and the person doesn't ask again.

You grab the diver and pull him inside, lock the door, close the windows, turn off the lights, and slump to the floor. This is where you begin your new life, the life where you wrestle to be rebirthed by this desperate, horrible night.

You steady your hands on the floor, feel the flatness, nothing moving or shifting, just a floor. You can do this. *Come on. You're you. You're me. It's me. She's there. You're here. I'm here. I'm here. I'm here.*

TWELVE

What happened? The diver forces me to look at him. My eyes go cold. What happened? he demands.

My mind cuts the final cord to emotion and wraps around the O. Henry story about the Christmas presents, the pocket watch and hair combs. He doesn't want to hear that story.

What happened?

Crouched on the floor of the cabana, I don't tell him that my body feels exhausted and sick, even my skin, even my hair. I tell him I took a long walk.

WHAT DID HE DO TO YOU?

I tell him he stole my money. I apologize for being late.

WHAT ELSE? WHAT DID HE DO?

I can't tell you.

You have to tell me.

I can't tell you.

I have to get my gun.

SOUVENIR SNAPSHOT. A jaguar, shot in the head, draped over the back of a motorcycle.

No! I pull at the diver's arm, beg him not to leave me alone. I crawl across the cabana to the bed, climb on it, and lay on my back. The diver towers over me.

Tell me.

My words are slow and deliberate. He stole my money.

And . . .

X.

The diver doesn't move. I don't move. We stare at each other. Neither of us knows what to do next. The diver moves first. He takes off my clothes, inspects me for injuries.

Then he pellets me with questions. What time did he pick me up? It's been hours, was I with him the entire time? Was I drinking? Did I struggle? Why didn't I say something on the porch? Why didn't I scream for help?

When the diver's satisfied I'm telling the truth, I have to decide if I will go to the police. Yes, no. I don't know what to do.

I lie on the bed agonizing and reeling. My adrenaline is crashing, surging, crashing, surging. *How can anyone make a decision in this state?* My heart is in my kneecaps, and my feet are in my teeth. I'm disoriented, out of proportion. I've been wrung like a wet sheet through a press. The people I know and trust are in a different country. I don't have a history with the diver. We don't know how to make decisions together. I want the diver's advice but he says no, I have to decide for myself. I want to call my friend in Los Angeles, but the diver's cell phone doesn't get reception in the cabana, and I'm afraid to walk to the payphone. *What if the jaguar man is waiting outside? What if he hurts me?*

There are two things I want most.

1. A shower.

2. To go home.

What the jaguar man did was wrong. I'm never confused about that. I know what everyone knows. X is criminal, monstrous. It's violent to the body and abrasive to the soul. Later, when I'm home, I'll be surrounded by people who want the jaguar man in jail or dead, butchered and skinned. His hide thrown on the floor like a rug. I don't want him to go unpunished, but right now I don't feel rage or the desire for revenge. I don't feel anything.

That's not true. I feel lingering compassion.

I feel lingering compassion.

If I report him, I will have to stay in the country. There are no medical kits or composite sketches in this tiny village. If I report him, I cannot take a shower until after I go to Belize City tomorrow and find a place where they collect DNA evidence. I will have to figure out the Belizean judicial system. If they catch him, I will have to face the jaguar man again. I will have to send him to jail.

I don't know the sentencing practices of Belize, but I figure if he's caught he'll be locked up for life. If I believed the courts would sentence him to counseling and rehabilitation, if I thought the system was restorative, I'd do it. But prison? I've always thought prison is an endless walk in hell, a place where the sickest people go only to get more pain inflicted on them in new ways, akin to treating blistering wounds by dousing them with battery acid. He needs to be held responsible, but how do I send someone to hell? I promised.

Later people will analyze me. Stockholm Syndrome. *Maybe,* I'll think. *Maybe.* But I will always maintain that my right as his victim is that I get treated, and *he* gets treated. He's profoundly sick and needs to get better. I will look up "victim's rights" online but I won't find this right expressed on any website. I will quickly discover I don't hold a popular opinion.

Later, I will become obsessed with questions about justice. I will wonder about the men and women sitting inside prisons all over the world. I will become friends with men who served time, some guilty and some wrongly convicted. I will be drawn to them. I will visit a prison, meet old-timers who have lived behind prison walls and barbed gates for twenty-five, thirty, thirty-five years, men who will continue living there until they die and are buried on prison grounds. Many of these men haven't held someone's hand or received a birthday call or an encouraging note in decades. How does a person survive? I will resent the hard questions the jaguar man has left me to consider. What does it mean for him to pay for his crime? What, and whom, does he owe?

These questions will come, but as I lie at the edge of the bed, I just want to go home. I know I should get medical attention, but there's only a small clinic here. I want to be checked by a licensed doctor in a big sterile hospital in my own city. I want to make the right decision, but I can't think straight. I want to take a shower and get the jaguar man off my skin.

But what if he does it again? What if he hurts someone else? It will be my fault.

It will be my fault.

I want to pretend it never happened and go to the caye with the diver in the morning, have a vacation, and fall in love. I want so many conflicting things and I don't know how to choose.

The diver wants to call his friends to hunt down the jaguar man on the road—island justice. I'm sure someone will end up dead. What if the diver dies? What if the jaguar man dies?

FACT. A jaguar caller can produce the grunt of either sex. Cut the top and bottom off a gourd, weave dried deerskin onto the top, and hang waxed string from the skin. Pull the string: one— pause—two. This is useful for hunting.

My mind tries to grab on to an answer, but my thoughts are like smoke rings. Then suddenly I think about *her.*

Her. The part of me still in the jungle. *Her.*

I promised the jaguar man silence. My rational mind knows that promise doesn't count. But my fear says if I betray him, he will track me down like he said he would. I don't believe him (but I do). He can't find me (but he can). He can find the helium part of me still in the jungle. He's the only one who knows where to look. If he finds her, he will take his knife and plunge it in her throat. I left her out there alone but I can't let his knife penetrate her skin.

It takes all my energy to get off the bed. I roll to my side, push myself up, stand, and steady myself to the bathroom. The cabana is dark. I flip the bathroom switch and flood the room with light, turn on the shower, let it warm, and step in. The diver follows me. It's cramped in the small space. I scrub my body, all the places the jaguar man touched—which is everywhere—but I can't feel the rough washcloth or the burn of soap or my skin rubbed raw.

After my shower I get dressed in the black lace lingerie I brought for the diver's birthday. I think I am strong for doing this. Later I will understand I am not strong. I am turned off, a switch cutting the connection between my own wires. The diver cries on the bed, and outside a sea wind howls onto shore. I sit next to him, pretty in lace, and force him to open his birthday presents a week early. It is not the time for this, but I will leave tomorrow and I'm determined to make this night meaningful with the diver. He turns the book of emails I made for him page by page. He cries, but I do not. The part of me that feels is hiding with the frogs, or she's trapped, or, God only knows, still caught by her hair in a tree. The diver holds my hand, but his kindness cannot reach me. I tell him not to worry about me; I'll be fine. I tie this lie into a knot that moors me, and it will be a long time before the fibers of the rope wear thin.

THIRTEEN

My eyes are open all night. I stare at the ceiling. I stare at the wall. I lay in the dark feeling sick. I haven't eaten, I can't sleep, my heart is breaking, and I'm in shock. The night is long. The diver wakes up several times and puts his hands on my face, whispers for me to sleep. He tells me in his deep voice he loves me. I say I love him, too. We say it over and over. I close my eyes and open them again. The jaguar man is inside my closed eyes.

I drift through the night, time is vague, the darkness is a vacuum sucking the dust mites of my thoughts. I lay on my side facing the diver. I barely move. If I'm hot or cold I don't notice. Hour by hour I float, puffs of wind shooing *her* in one direction, me in the other.

Then it's morning. I need to go home but I don't want to leave the diver. He says go, he'll see me soon, don't worry. He'll apply again for a United States visa, it's sure to be accepted this time. There's no reason to deny the visa, but these are days of terrorists and closed borders, and even though he's a gentle man of the sea, he's still considered *other*. He promises to find a way to see me again, we'll meet in a neutral country, but I need to go home.

My stomach aches as I drop things in my suitcase. Not everything, though. I leave my hat with the leather string cut off. I leave the flip-flops I was wearing. I leave incidental clothes and toiletries I'm too tired to pack. I close my suitcase and wait for the diver to return with a taxi. I ask him to please double check it's a real taxi, get one with a driver he knows. He says don't worry, he'll ride with me, he has to go to work and he'll drop me off at the airstrip on his way. This was supposed to be our day to go to his private caye, where he would fix moorings while I relaxed and swam. He's still going to work. I don't understand this choice. *Isn't what happened important enough to call off work?*

My plane ticket says I'm leaving in eleven days. I can get a flight to Belize City from the tiny village but I don't know if I can get a flight out of Belize City to Los Angeles today. I'd rather not be alone, but I don't ask him to come with me. I don't ask him for what I need. I don't want to impose, and he didn't offer. Plus, I don't get the sense he'll say yes and I can't bear to hear no. I tell him I'll be fine.

It's 7:10 A.M. He puts my suitcase in the taxi and sits with me in the back. It takes three minutes to get to the airstrip, and there's a twelve-passenger plane about to depart to the international airport in Belize City. The diver speaks in Creole to the person at the counter who rolls my suitcase across the airstrip to the plane. I pay my money for a ticket. It all happens fast. The plane is preparing to leave. I have to say goodbye to the diver. I don't want to go. He hugs me.

I look at the clock. It's 7:15 A.M. I have to get on the plane. I walk across the airstrip and turn to look at the diver who has turned to look at me. We both turn back our separate ways. I get on the plane. I haven't eaten since lunch yesterday. I haven't slept. I'm on a little plane with three other people heading away from this place I thought would change my life for the better. It's hot in the plane. I rest my head against the window and tell myself to breathe. *In. Out. In. Out.* I concentrate on the basics. *Breathe.*

The plane arrives in Belize City at 8:00 A.M. before the ticket counters open. I have to wait until 8:30 A.M. for check-in. Thirty minutes. I stare at the clock. I sit on a hard bench facing the counter and stare at the stanchions that mark short aisles. I stare at the counter. I picture the diver on a boat heading to his island. Tears collect in my eyes. Time passes in slow motion.

Finally, a woman in a uniform emerges from behind the counter and motions to me. My voice cracks that I need to get on the first plane to Los Angeles. The tears I've been holding back stream down my cheeks at the mention of home. I cry but all I feel is exhaustion. I wonder if she senses X. She doesn't ask why I'm crying or if I need help, but she can change my ticket for $100. Credit card. One suitcase. Pay exit fee at the security counter. Here's the boarding pass. The plane leaves at 3:55 P.M. It arrives in Houston at 7:30 P.M., where there's a three-hour layover. The flight to Los Angeles lands at midnight.

I look at the clock. 8:35 A.M. Through the fog in my mind I count. Seven hours until I leave Belize. Sixteen hours until I'm home, plus the time difference, seventeen hours. I look at the clock. 8:36 A.M.

I picture the diver on a boat heading toward the caye without me. I wonder what he's thinking. I want to hear his voice. I have enough money on an old calling card to call the diver, but his cell phone doesn't have reception on the boat so I leave a message saying I arrived at the airport safely, I miss him, and I hope he has a beautiful day.

My responsible mind tells me to eat. I walk upstairs to the café and order the American breakfast without bacon or sausage, just two eggs and two pieces of toast, water, and orange juice. The waitress says the American breakfast comes with meat. I don't want sausage or bacon; the thought of meat makes me queasy. I repeat I'd like the American breakfast without the meat and don't mind if it's still the same price. I sit alone at a small, brown, tiled table that faces the runway. The waitress yells my order across the kitchen. "No meat! No meat!" There are other people in the restaurant, but I barely see them.

I stare at the sign that advertises xocóatl, traditional hot chocolate. On the table is a drink menu in a plastic stand. Virgin fun drinks. Local brews and sodas. Fun drinks with alcohol. On the back of the menu are instructions to pray before I eat. It suggests a prayer in case I don't know how to pray or if I don't want to think of my own. "We give thee thanks, Almighty God, for these and all the blessings which we receive from thy bounty. Through Christ our

Lord. Amen." It's written in English and Spanish. I stare at it, words on a page.

I want a banana from the big basket, a yellow one, not brown, but the waitress won't sell bananas, they're for fruit shakes. Thoughts cross my mind without catching, and the bananas are forgotten. I stare out the window, tears in my eyes, until the waitress brings my food and a plastic fork and knife. I stand up, walk to the trashcan and throw away the knife.

I walk back across the café, return to my seat, and spread grape jelly on the burnt toast with a fork. I eat one bite of egg—it's heavy, mud, muck from the earth—I eat another bite, force myself to swallow. The juice burns my throat. My stomach aches. I don't know what time it is when I finish eating. Let's say 8:55 A.M.

I move outside to a wooden bench, using my backpack as a pillow. The bench is hard, tears in my eyes. I watch men walk by my bench. *Has he X? Has he? Has he? The man holding his son's hand. Has he? The man in the hat? The one leaning against the rail?* My mind plays this guessing game until I notice and force myself to stop.

RIDDLE. If one in six women experiences X, how many men does it take to X one in six women?

My friend. I need to call my friend. I practice in my mind telling her what happened, the words are jumbled, the words don't make sense, I feel nauseous from exhaustion, and I want to be home. It's 9:15 A.M., 8:15 A.M. in Los Angeles where my friend teaches summer school; the day already started, she'll be hard to reach. I walk across the street to the office that sells phone cards, ten minutes for BZ$20.

Has he X?

Has he?

I walk back across the street to the pay phones and dial. It doesn't work, no international signal. I carefully read the directions on the card and try again. It rings. Her cell phone is off, voice mail. She's with her class and won't turn her phone back on until this afternoon, but I can't wait that long. I have to talk to her right now. Now. I work at the same school. I know everybody there, I know the schedule, I call the main office, tell my coworker who answers that I'm in Belize, it's an emergency, I ask him to cover her class, tell her to take her cell phone to a place on campus where she can have a private conversation, to do this right now, I can't wait. I have five minutes left on the calling card. I need more time. I go across the street to the office, buy another card, ten minutes for BZ$20. Cross back to the phones. It's 9:30 A.M. I dial my friend's number, and she answers.

What's wrong? What's going on?

I tell her I'm coming home. My voice is steady now. I tell her my time with the diver was fine, he's not the problem. Yesterday a man pretending to be a cab driver drove me to the jungle and X. I tell her he had a knife. I don't hear her reaction. I listen to myself talk as though I'm someone else, someone outside me. Everything is disconnected. I ask her if she will pick me up at the airport and take me to the hospital for treatment. I think that's what I should do. Will she call the hospital and find out if there's anything else, anything that I should do right now, before I get home? I took a shower, washed away the evidence but what about HIV, I want to take care of business, will she meet me at the airport, will she take tomorrow off and stay with me, I might not want to be alone. The time on the calling card is running out. Yes, yes, she'll do everything I asked. She'll stay with me as long as I need. I hang up the phone, take a deep breath, walk inside, and look at the clock. It's 9:39 A.M.

I go to the restroom, stand in front of the mirror. I don't look like I should. I should have bruises and cuts on my arms and legs and stomach and back and feet and genitals. I should be bloody and broken. There should be a knife sticking out of my stomach. My hair should be seaweed, and my teeth should be dirt. There should be gashes that will one day be scars. *It's strange there's no injury that will scar.* There's not a mark on me. The branches and thorns didn't scratch, the mosquitoes and sand flies didn't bite.

How is that possible?

I splash my face with water, put my hair in a ponytail, and walk back to the wooden bench. I sit and stare at the runway. A plane is leaving or coming. It doesn't matter; it's not my plane. I stare at it, but nothing registers. I watch people move around the plane. *Has he X?* I check the clock and tell myself not to, it doesn't help, it won't make time go faster.

The book about the boy and the tiger is in my backpack. I take it out and read a sentence, but the words scratch my eyes. I put the book away, walk around the tiny airport, inside, outside, inside, outside, return to the office that sells phone cards, and buy another ten minutes for BZ$20 so I can call my friend again later.

I try to remember what happened, but my mind shuts down. It should hurt to remember, hurt like jagged glass pushed through my veins or lungs collapsing in salt, but I don't feel a thing. The part of me that feels is abandoned by the sea. I left her there to deal with her pain alone. She's probably hiding under leaves and sand, terrified of every sound, screaming for someone to help. I don't like her and I flick her away.

I walk through the airport, move my arms and legs by habit, past the pay phones, past the wooden benches, past the café, past the ticket counter, upstairs, downstairs. It's 9:58 A.M. Inside, outside, inside, outside. I buy a bottle of water then browse the T-shirts and shot glasses and key chains and wood carvings of jaguars in the store. It's 10:03 A.M. I walk slowly, go through this door, past that door, back in, out, a guard watches. I nod as I walk by, he nods back, he stands near the phones, maybe he heard my conversation, maybe he saw me cry. *How am I going to get through this day, how am I going to make it to 3:55 P.M.?* I'm flushed, maybe I have a fever. I walk into the air-conditioned lobby and sit on a chair. I tell myself I'm okay. The worst is over. Nothing else is going to happen to me.

My mind flashes micro-thoughts. The man's dark hair. His red bandana. I shift in the wooden chair, and my thoughts shutter. *Where is he right now? Is he thinking about me? What did he do this morning? Did he wake up early or late? Did he eat tortillas and eggs for breakfast? Linger over a cup of hot coffee? Is he in the jungle or the city? Is he on the run? Does he have an image of me locked in his mind? What does he remember? The length of my hair? My blue eyes? My name? Where is the van? Where is the knife? Did he spend my money?*

I close my eyes and see the snarled patch of trees and vines where pieces of me were left to take root. I see the red polish partially scraped off his left thumb. Click. I hear him lock the passenger door. My mind blurs the sharp edge of the knife. I wonder if I'm abstract parts, a broken shadow to him like he is to me. I concentrate but I can't picture him in specifics. His face is gone, his height vanished, his weight evaporated. I can't even recall the exact color of the van. His distinguishing features are already barred and banned behind my mind's steel doors, the doors padlocked, chained, and guarded with snarling dogs ready to attack.

I spend the day minute by minute. Read a sentence in my book and stop.

Flash. Red polish, straw hat.

I sip on water and replace the cap.

Flash. Knife, bandana, diver, sky.

I call my friend at lunchtime, 12:05 P.M. She confirms the nurse said come straight to the hospital tonight; don't wait until tomorrow. I hang up the phone. Sit on the bench. Nod to the guard. *Has he X?* Buy plantain chips and eat them slowly. Rearrange magnets and mugs in the store. Wait. Breathe. Check the clock. I put my head on my backpack and sleep for ten minutes. People walk up the ramp onto their planes, happy and rested after their vacations. People walk down the ramp and wave to family and friends. I put on a sweater when I'm inside the air conditioning and take it off when I'm outside in the heat. Drink water. Stretch legs and gently massage neck. Wait. I get used to the fog in my mind and how I can't feel any emotion. I get used to the clock moving slowly. I get used to the guard who watches me. I get used to the idea that this same backpack was with me yesterday in the van.

Finally, finally I board my plane. When I arrive in Houston, I exit the plane, follow the lines, follow the rules of customs, show my passport, thank the customs officer who welcomes me back, collect my suitcase at carousel twelve, hand in my declaration form, and drop the suitcase off at the conveyor belt for connecting flights. I take the escalator upstairs, follow the line through the maze for the security check, take off my shoes, remove my sweater, keep moving, follow the line, put shoes back on, wrap sweater around my waist, check for the correct gate, step on the moving sidewalk, go to the other end of the terminal, keep moving, follow the signs, stop in the bathroom, look in the mirror and pale tired tears well up in my eyes but I hold them back. I arrive at the gate then wait, two hours until I board the flight and four hours in the air to Los Angeles. I'm almost home.

My friend is at the airport in Los Angeles. I smile. She inhales relief. She spent the day imagining I was beaten and bruised, but I'm unmarked. She gives me a big hug, and I tell her a trivial story about the plane. I offer to pay for parking and ask her about her day, but, no, she's not going to talk. She needs to hear what happened.

I tell her the details of the jaguar man as she drives east on the 105 freeway, which takes us to the 110 North, then the 101 North to the exit nearest my house so I can wash my face, brush my teeth, and get my HMO card before I go to the hospital. I highlight the good parts of X: how I didn't get stabbed, how my mind was clear, how I responded with compassion, how compassion seemed appropriate, how I think compassion saved my life, how I prayed and two lights appeared out of the sea just in time, a bus with no sound and no form. I'm not even sure it was a bus, now that I think of it, how could it be a bus? The compassion and the lights and the man with the knife didn't confuse me until now.

I notice faint screams from the part of me still in Belize, the part wildly trying to escape the thin stretch of beach I left her on, but I tune her out, don't mention her to my friend. Instead, I focus on describing how I got away unharmed.

The emergency room is full but not crowded. I tell the nurse about X and after I settle the $35 copayment with my remaining traveler's cheque, she escorts me quickly to the examining room. I tell her I took a shower and I know I ruined the evidence, but I'm worried about HIV and other STDs. A male doctor comes in, the female nurse stays, and my friend stays.

I put my feet in the stirrups, legs spread apart, knees fall to both sides. The examining room is cold, and the metal speculum he uses to examine my vaginal canal is cold, but my body has not registered pain since the moment the jaguar man pointed his knife into my skin, so I don't feel any physical sensations other than cold when he inserts the long nose of the speculum or widens it to check the vaginal walls and swab my cervix. No internal injuries. No external injuries. No visible signs of violence.

The doctor and nurse move aside to have a hushed conversation. When they return, we decide not to call the police because X occurred in another country. The doctor and nurse both scurry around the emergency room trying to find an informative brochure of helpful agencies. The doctor flips through the hefty Yellow Pages phone book but doesn't find a number he thinks could be useful. My friend looks at me and rolls her eyes. I wonder why they're not trained in available resources.

I don't know it yet, but this is just the beginning of a frustrating experience with a dysfunctional social service network. They suggest I call my primary care physician in the morning for follow up tests and referrals. The nurse prepares samples and draws blood for base tests that will indicate if I already have gonorrhea, syphilis, chlamydia, hepatitis A or B, or HIV. I know I'm clean; I'm not worried about these results. I'm worried about the results in three months. The nurse asks questions about X in order to determine if she should administer a highly toxic HIV cocktail as preventive medicine. She decides not to. It's rare to contract the virus that way, extremely remote, because there was no exchange of blood. I repeat back to her: extremely remote. She gives me large doses of antibiotics for gonorrhea, syphilis, and chlamydia, a vaccination against hepatitis B, and emergency contraception.

Antibiotics always make me ill, and the nurse warns I'll get very sick from these. I'm nauseous almost immediately, stomach contracting like fists, so while my friend fills the prescription for more pills at the all-night pharmacy, I wait in the car and vomit into a plastic bag. It occurs to me to be afraid, alone in a dark corner of the parking garage in the middle of the night but I'm too sick, too beyond my own mind to move somewhere lit. I vomit several times before my friend returns, and several more times on the way home, each time my friend pulls over to the side of the road. By the time I get home there's nothing left in my stomach, but I dry heave in the bathroom.

My friend brings the yellow comforter and down pillow from my bed, and I curl on the bathroom floor facing the toilet. Another friend who's a professional muralist had helped paint mermaids on the bathroom wall, and now I look up at them from the floor, buoyed above me, floating on their painted sea. When the nausea passes, I brush my teeth. I've been awake for forty-two hours. I drag the comforter and pillow to bed where I sleep, deeply. My friend is next to me, my house is locked, I'm countries away from the jaguar man, there's medicine in my body that will kill several forms of STDs, I won't get pregnant, and I'm not alone. It's 4:00 A.M., and I've done all I can do today.

FOURTEEN

MYTH. The jaguar man drives his van on the dirt road out of the village, pushes the gas pedal to the floor, and lurches forward. It's dark, no streetlights. He has to get out of here, go far away, leave the country, he'll never come back. He'll get his son and take the boy with him. He's not going to live without his son. He has American dollars now and his knife. He has momentum. He can take his son, he'll crush whoever gets in his way if he has to, he'll start over somewhere else, Guatemala, Honduras, he'll put his cheek against the ground, plant himself like a seed, he'll become a different man.

Where the hell is he going to go? Hide in the forest like it's a holy shrine? Perch like a hawk in the treetops? He should never have trusted the tourist. The police are probably already on the road. He should have killed her, deboned her like a fish, at least left her back there so he could get a head start. What has he done?

He speeds, out of control on the snake bends of the road. There is only one way in and out of the village; he has to drive the reverse of what he has just driven with her. He was an outlaw before, now what is he, he wonders. He's a dead man. He'll die misunderstood, like a kiss, like the sun in hell. She can identify him, she knows his voice and face, he told her his name, the man in the hammock saw him, he was too nice to her, he should never have let her go.

He drives past Maya Beach, and the engine sputters, out of gas. Frantic, he gathers everything he owns, stuffs his pockets with his wallet, knife, lighter, and the crumpled traveler's cheque the woman left behind. He doesn't know how to get rid of her scent, her DNA, and his, their lives spilled and crisscrossed on the vinyl seats. He crushes fistfuls of dirt and leaves over the seats and doors, the places she touched. He stabs the seats with his knife, makes a violent mess. He makes things worse. He always makes things worse.

He runs along the edge of the road, foot, paw, foot, paw, dizzy with this new language of running. Even if he can't see the road in the dark, he can feel the pocked dirt under his feet to guide him. When he's out of breath, he slows to a walk, what else can he do? If this is his night to die, he'll die. He should have hanged himself in the sanctuary on the tree, let Balam devour him later.

FACT. In trauma, mammals tremble and shake until they regain their balance and neutralize their response.

He senses someone behind him. He holds the handle of his knife and spins around. No one is there. He has to calm down. He needs a plan and a way out. Grow wings. Turn to liquid. Find an inner fold in his fucked-up life. He walks and hears footsteps behind him, step by step. He knows it's the police. He has to make a choice. He can't go to jail. Should he run or fight? The footsteps get closer. Footsteps in the dark are eerie. When he was little, Abu held his hand when they walked at night. He's not little anymore. He'll bite through the skull of fear and meet his fate. He turns again and sees the tourist. It's her.

What is she doing on the road behind him? He lunges at her with his knife. He'll get rid of her this time. He's not taking any chances. He grabs her with his left hand, holds her arm. She doesn't resist. He plunges his knife into her neck with his right hand, and the knife easily sinks in. She smiles at him, a look of pity. He sends the knife through her again, this time into her chest, her heart. Again and again and again, he's a madman with his knife. She stands and gives him that half smile, a moon, a cradle. She never loses her footing. He grunts and spits saliva with the effort of his attack. She doesn't bleed or cry or change expression. He backs away from her and runs, off the road, on the road, off the road, on the road, he zigzags a maniacal path. He turns and there she is, slow and calm. No matter how quickly he runs, she is right behind him.

His stomach heaves. He falls, his hands and knees on the ground, a churning deep in his gut. It seems as though everything he's eaten since he was born comes up, milk, mangoes, tortillas, and fish, along with all his lost questions, whys and whens, his young loves that broke like shattered mirrors, the blue butterflies of his heart, the spider nests of his youth, the rebellions of his marriage, everything inside him pulled up from its fleshy roots.

He gags and vomits and retches then curls on the side of the road next to his own waste and prays that this is death. She sits on a rock a short distance away and watches him purge.

FACT. Watching something happen changes the way it happens. The more you observe, the greater the effect.

He curls into a tighter ball, a pain in his head louder than the one in his stomach. When he can stand again, he stands. When he finds his balance again and can walk, he walks. She walks beside him.

A bar appears on the side of the road. The door opens. He enters, sits at a small table in the corner, and orders a Belikin and a shot. It burns his raw throat and the lining of his stomach. Another shot. Another Belikin. Another. She stands in the center of the bar and watches him drink. No police on the road. No one else in the bar. So this is his fate, he thinks. *She'll follow me wherever I go.*

At some time during the night he passes out. He wakes up on the sand. How did he get here, he wonders? The sun is the blazing eye of the sky's tender face. He sits up, checks his pockets. Empty. His wallet is gone, his knife is gone, even his lighter and the crumbled traveler's cheque. He wipes his mouth on the back of his hand. Now what is he going to do? He knows he has done bad things. He knows bad things will keep happening to him in life and after death; it's natural law.

He crawls, like a wild animal, to the shade of a palm tree, looks out toward the sea and there she is, in front of him, that expression of pity. As panic rises in his chest again, she slowly takes the form of Balam—multi-colored, shimmering with a gold underbelly, sleek, and strong. What did the jaguar man expect? Not this. Balam steps closer and looks down at the man with the saddest eyes. The man turns away. Balam scrapes the sand to mark he was there.

Six feet tail to nose, power and grace. The sight of Balam undoes him.

The wind picks up from the east. A storm brews, this time of year there's always a storm, and the man braces himself against the tree. When the sky pummels him with rain, the man turns his face from the beating and cries. The rain pounds like ancient temple stones against his skull.

Balam stands under the tree with the man. Balam, his son, his wife who used to love him and who he still loves, the tourist, and what his life could have been. All under the tree with him in the rain.

This is real pain, he thinks, *this sadness and regret. Nothing more horrible than the pain that comes from your own choices in life.*

FIFTEEN

For the next forty-eight hours, I replay X many times. Why not? It's not my fault. No shame. My friend sits beside me at my kitchen table while I make call after call. I think if I don't tell people right away it will be awkward later, for them or me, or both. I dread the phone calls but get a certain satisfaction being in control. I want order, authority, and no surprises. I become expert at telling the story, a short version for family, a slightly extended one for friends. I control the narrative, edit the details I think might upset people most, choosing my words carefully and insisting I got away unharmed. My parents, sisters, and brother converge at my home. They fly in from their respective cities so we can be together as a family. They hug me and reassure me (and themselves) that I'm okay. Everyone I tell—family, friends, colleagues—responds with kindness and concern, and discomfort. X becomes a one-conversation topic that isn't brought up again, unless by me.

The diver reports X to the resort, and I'm relieved when he says someone will post warning signs.

I'm grateful, yes, but I feel no exuberance at being alive.

SOUVENIR SNAPSHOT. Jaguar piñata hanging from a tree. Beside it, a woman poised to bash it with a stick.

MYTH. The jaguar man creeps to his ex-wife's house and shines a stolen flashlight through the window, a signal to his son. He waits in the weeds, a long time for nothing. All he wants is to see the boy. Goddamn, can't he just see his boy?

I tell only select friends about the bus, how its lights appeared out of nowhere when the jaguar man was fiercest, how I silently prayed. I think about those lights over and over. What were they? A bus couldn't come from the sea, that doesn't make sense, and a bus never passed on the abandoned road. The lights melted into darkness as quickly as they appeared. What were the lights? It seemed odd then, but it's baffling now.

What does *he* think they were?

And what about how I held the man's hand, prayed over him, and wished him many blessings at the end of the night? Why did I do that? What part of me was in charge? Where is that part now? I prayed for an experience of love so big I'd have to change my life to comprehend it. Is this the awful answer to my prayer?

TRUTH. Compassion has impact but no physical mass. It's hard to hold the air, the weightlessness, of it steady.

VOICE NUMBER 1. Why didn't you report him?

Even as I recount the experience over and over, I can feel it slipping away, so I write down everything I remember as precisely as I can. But memory has limits. Already my memory is hazy about specific details. I'm sure the jaguar man had dark hair but I can't describe his eyes or nose or mouth. I know he was wearing a red bandana.

Soon I will tell someone his bandana was blue, and it will sound vaguely wrong. I will go back to my notes and discover my mistake. I will find that some details are locked tight in my mind, and others are already riding the fluid, changing nature of memory. I spent all those hours with the jaguar man, just the two of us face to face, but I'm already an unreliable witness.

I've blocked so much out, yet I want to know more. I want to know his story, the parts before and after my encounter with him, which I wasn't there to witness, thank God. He becomes territory for my imagination. What led him that day to me? What did he want? Not money, no. What did he *really* want, his deep-down cave-cold urge? What did he attempt to soothe in him by harming me?

I play detective with the clues he left for me. If I understand him, I might understand X. If I understand X, I might understand the nature of compassion. Compassion for the jaguar man saved my life, stilled his pounding, lowered his knife. Compassion rearranged my landscape, and his, like patterns in beads and broken glass. If I understand compassion, I might understand how getting caught in his pain could actually grow me in ways that I (say it) will appreciate.

So I keep looking at him from different angles and in tilted mirrors. He takes on peculiar new shapes, morphs into myth, and grows powerful legs and a sleek jaguar coat. My mind finds ways to make sense of things.

VOICE NUMBER 2. Why didn't you report him?

There's still one room in my house that needs a new floor. It becomes unbearable to live with the hideous tattered carpet in the small guest room. I want it fixed. Now. In a burst of energy, I tear out the carpet and underneath I discover hundreds of small nails bent in the painted wood.

I start pulling up nails, grab at them like rotten teeth with the pronged side of a miniature hammer. One by one, I yank them out until there are piles of old nails, so many they stack on top of each other and take the form of a man, starting from the feet and building up to the head, even the face, even his hair. A man made of rusty nails. Nails pulled from private places. Nails once sticking out of wood are now sticking out of him. Nails that are bent. Nails that were never hammered properly. The man is a skeleton of these old mangled mistakes. A man in the shape of a man, but who is not a man. A man made of stabbing, jabbing, and forcing things together—things that are meant to be apart. Nails for eyes. Nails for words. His breath hissing around its own sharp point. Nails that drove down deep where they never belonged, where they had no permission to go.

FACT. One in six women.

That's the statistic in the United States today. What will it be tomorrow?

One in six women fights back or doesn't fight back, screams or doesn't scream, scratches a man's eyes, kicks his groin, walks in the middle of the street under the light, runs, pleads, doesn't drink alone in bars, or does, doesn't dress provocatively, or does, goes to workshops, takes a self-defense course, doesn't trust strangers, or does, feels confident, acts aware, holds her keys between her fingers, arms herself with mace, or locks doors behind her. And then what? None of that matters if he has a knife, an aggression, a demand, a pain, a sickness, a disconnection, a brutal need he, he, the man, *he* never learned to handle.

One in six. And less than half report it.

VOICE NUMBER 3. Why didn't you report him?

Something's obviously not working for women (and men). Women (and men) understandably don't want to face the questioning (and blame) inherent in the reporting process. Women (and men) might not want the perpetrator, who they often know, to go to prison. Accountability, yes, but what are the options?

I think in these detached abstracts; the reel of my mind lets out a line. Experts say X is about power. I think of the jaguar man, and the statement seems incomplete. Power to do what? Connect? Get his son? Soothe his rage? Belong where he feels cut off? Force himself in?

Whatever it is, it's an epidemic. These sick men could fill the hospitals of the world. They're self-medicating through means of X.

Do they recognize that what they inflict on others they also inflict on themselves? They need test tubes and research, a vaccination, a cure. Someone needs to discover the tsetse fly that carries their disease. They need to speak up and explain themselves.

Who is dealing with these men?

SOUVENIR SNAPSHOT. A jaguar pelt stretched between bamboo rods for sale on the side of the road.

MYTH. I'm in charge. I send a thousand of these sick men into the woods. Not to exact terror and revenge. Not to incite chaos and violence. No, these woods heal and shock. *Oh, this is how it feels to be well. This is how it feels to be loved. This is how it feels to respect myself and others.* I send a thousand of these men into the woods. I tell them, stay there and don't come back until you have a plan for fixing other men like you.

My foot taps the floor. I'm cold and clinical. I can analyze but why can't I feel? It happened years ago, in a faraway place, to someone else, a woman, a ghost floating nearby, hard to catch, not me, someone I know, a good friend, not me, not on Sunday, today's Wednesday, not three days ago. I should still be on vacation with the diver, the one who lives in that hell paradise, the one who's there and not here.

I get a referral for a psychologist, PhD, who specializes in trauma. My friend drives me to the appointment in a fancy building in a ritzy part of town. I immediately distrust her. She looks like a bleached Barbie doll—too much plastic surgery—a woman refusing to age. I follow her into her office where she's required to lay prone in her leather chair because she's had some sort of sinus or back surgery (I wasn't listening, I was distracted by her fake nose and breasts), and she's uncomfortable if she sits straight up. She instructs me to tell her what happened. I do, in detail. I mention the bus, and she wheezes through her throat, which makes me think her problem is sinus. She listens dutifully and watches the clock. My story takes nearly an hour. At the end, I express concern that I can't feel any emotion. She deepens her recline and suggests I wear an elastic band around my wrist, snap it whenever X seems unreal or far away. Snap myself out of it.

I hate this psychologist's stupid advice, hate it even more when she tells me her fee, which is twice what I expected. I forgot to ask about money when I made the appointment and now I'm suddenly seething. I feel the urge to pull her bleached hair out of her Barbie head and pop her fake breasts with a crochet hook. I don't have money to waste, which is what I did. She wants to make another appointment. I imagine if I snap an elastic band like a sling shot I can hit her tender sinus. I tell her I can't afford her rates, and she offers to let her intern treat me for half the price. She'll monitor the case, a special deal for me. Her voice whines from between her unnaturally plump lips.

A tiny speck of stillness inside me grabs hold. I politely tell her I'll call if I change my mind. I politely see myself out. I leave a trail of polite anger as I walk down the hallway, relieved if I can't feel emotion about X then I can at least feel disgust toward her.

We get in the car and my friend drives me across town to my church, a progressive Catholic church with a progressive priest, the only reason I'm still trying to stay Catholic. The receptionist doesn't make appointments for the priest; I have to call him personally. I stand behind the counter and explain that I need immediate counseling, mentioning X to get her attention. She's annoyed I'm still in the office when she clearly told me to go home and call the priest. I walk outside, call him on my cell phone from the rectory steps, and leave a message. It takes two messages and several days for him to respond.

Later, on another day, my sister will tell me about Saint Maria Goretti, virgin martyr of purity. My sister read about Saint Maria in her Catholic primer in grade school and, so disturbed, never forgot her. I research the story and discover Maria Goretti was eleven years old when an older boy attempted to rape her. She fought him, warned him he'd go to hell, and for refusing to submit he stabbed her fourteen times with a knife. In the hours of suffering before she died, she forgave him as she received last rites and held her gaze on an image of the Blessed Mother. The boy was sentenced to thirty years in prison and while imprisoned had a vision in which Maria met him in a garden and handed him white lilies. Because of that vision, he repented. The Catholic Church canonized Maria not only because she forgave the boy and her forgiveness reached beyond life into death, but also because she fought him in order to avoid sin, his and hers. Yes, his *and* hers. She was concerned for his soul and wanted him to join her in heaven. And she preferred death to the dishonor of losing her purity and virginity, which would have offended God.

Offended God? Patron saint of purity, young girls, and victims of rape? Pope Pius XII, who presided at her canonization in 1950, encouraged young girls to look to Maria for inspiration. Times have changed and I'm not a young girl, but there is nothing inspiring or comforting to me about this child choosing to die for her purity, nor anything commendable about a religion considering a girl who is raped to be in offense. What slick trick of faith is this?

Days go by, the sun, the moon, why can't I feel? The splintered part of me left by the sea claws at invisible walls. I'm not whole. I crave sleep and more sleep, all I want to do is sleep. But I return to work, answer phone calls and emails, efficient, responsible. There's a problem emerging at my job. The arts program I founded several years ago is no longer supported by the new administration. I sit in meetings, defend my program, try to find new sources of funding, but I'm asked to dismantle what I've spent years creating until it fits into their newly defined parameters. They know about X and say if I need time off I should take it; this is supposed to be my vacation. But I'm afraid if I'm not at work they'll decide the program's fate without me. I set an alarm clock each night, pull myself out of bed each morning, take a shower, drive to work, like a zombie, but I show up.

I get my period. It's soothing and womanly, alive, plump. It gives me a little lift to feel feminine, my body reclaiming itself. I empty out the suitcase that's been sitting on my bedroom floor. I put the clothes I was wearing in a bag. The bikini, T-shirt, shorts. I'll deal with those clothes in a year when I ritually burn them in a friend's fire pit, but for now I drive them around. They're tied in a white plastic grocery bag in the trunk of my car.

My friend wants to surprise her husband by redecorating their bedroom. I go shopping with her, get caught up in colors and textures. We have fun for an afternoon, and I forget about the jaguar man. My friend is one of the only people I want to be around, everyone else exhausts me. Most of the time I'm a high functioning robot moving my arms and legs by habit, taking deep breaths when I get winded from drawing shallow air.

I'm supposed to be a bridesmaid in a wedding next week. I tell the bride what happened, but she doesn't offer me an out and I don't have the heart to cancel, so I go through the motions, help her with last minute planning, attend the rehearsal dinner and wedding, and smile at the people I've never met, which is most of them. I want to crawl under the table, wrap myself up in a silk brocaded scarf like a cocoon. I wish to be small, invisible, and alone.

The jaguar man is still in me. I can sense the tension inside, like a conch shell, dried and scooped of its meat, still vibrating the sound of the sea. I pay my bills, buy groceries, and swim laps at the YMCA while he's trapped in my right shoulder and right hip. He's a barnacle, thorn, parasite, weed. Why can't I feel? How do I click back on the knob to my emotions? My house is loud, screams at me through the TV and radio. I turn everything off, sit in silence. I eat when I remember to. My friend's gone home. I tell her I'm fine. I tell the diver I'm fine.

You're the strongest woman I've ever met, the diver says. Anger makes people think and do things that make matters worse. I'm upset, but the sea is healing and I'm going on with my life.

I finally meet with the priest in the rectory. The priest listens to my story, admits he feels inadequate to help because he's not a woman; therefore, he can't relate. I assure him he doesn't need to be a woman, but he can help me understand the experience from a spiritual perspective. I ask him about the bus. Was it a miracle? Does God work that way? I wonder why everything was clear at the time, now it's cloudy and confused. He's uncomfortable, says something about Jesus and the resurrection. He looks at the clock. I watch his growing unease. His fluffy white dog wags into the room, and he gives it his attention. Pet the dog, pet the dog, don't look at me, pet the dog. He asks if there's anything else he can do for me, but I can tell he doesn't want an answer and I'm swept out the door without an offer to see me again.

I walk outside into the perfect California day and absolve myself from being Catholic. I've been hanging on by habit and hope but today I let go. If even the most progressive priest doesn't have the tools to deal with real life, if Catholic teachings don't have practical applications, this isn't the path for me. I'm too tired to make excuses for the church's failings. I walk down the sidewalk to my car.

I return a call from my sister in another state. She gives me information about a treatment center with one of the best reputations in the country. I've never heard of it, and no one has mentioned it even though it's in my city. I make an appointment for the next day. My counselor is calm and kind, and I appreciate that the services are free. She says I've already gone through enough and shouldn't be charged to heal.

I ask the counselor, Was it bad?

All X is bad, obviously. But still, I want to know about *mine*.

She says it has elements that make it one of the worst she's heard in her years of counseling. Kidnapping, weapon, bondage, foreign country, two aggravated assaults, fear of death, isolation, and prolonged encounter with the perpetrator.

Is she sure? It doesn't feel as bad as it sounds. I can hardly relate to the details of the night. It's muscle detached from tendon, tendon jerked from bone.

She wants to know, Do you have nightmares?

No.

Flashbacks?

No.

Afraid to be alone?

No.

Shame, embarrassment, anger, guilt?

No, no, no, no.

Considering buying a weapon?

No.

Difficulty sleeping?

No.

I want to meet other women, but the center doesn't have group sessions. Many women feel ashamed or are afraid to be further victimized. I think that's even more reason to have group sessions, but I don't express my opinion.

I don't know it yet, but for the next few years I will be drawn to women (and men) who will tell me their stories of X. We will somehow find each other. Our skin must smell of it. But today I tell the counselor I don't feel like a victim.

How do you feel? she wants to know.

I feel sorry for him.

I feel sorry for him.

That's about him, she replies. How do you feel about you?

I feel splintered, split in two.

I feel splintered, split in two. There and here, then and now, me and her.

I ask her, Where do you think I'm holding the memories, and where are my emotions?

Every woman responds in her own way.

How should I talk to people who are uncomfortable, who say Y instead of X, or don't say anything at all?

People will respond differently. You can't push them.

I'm quickly learning. Don't say X. Don't say X. Don't say X. Don't say X. No one wants to hear that shit.

I ask her to recommend a book and I buy it the same day. My counselor says the book is very good, but I disagree. The author details the ways X ruined her life. She's spent years in recovery and she's not recovered yet. This makes me alert. The jaguar man has been disruptive, but dear God please don't let him ruin my life. I figure I'll give myself a few weeks to restabilize then put this whole thing aside. Done, check that off the list. Seriously? Seriously.

I tell myself my life is bigger than what he can touch.

My life is bigger than what he can touch.

I tell my counselor my instinct is that X can somehow push me to a better life. I tell her about my prayer for a love so big I'll have to change my life to comprehend it. I tell her I'm confused by the compassion I felt, and still feel, for the jaguar man. I tell her I feel affixed to him, hooked in, connected. It feels like we're push and pull, or give and take.

FACT. The trunk of the Give-and-Take Palm is covered in poisonous thorns. The most effective antidote is from the tree's own inner bark.

Together the jaguar man and I went into the jungle beside the Caribbean Sea, and somehow together we emerged. What happened in that furtive corner of the world—a place so remote that even as I tell its story it seems to streak like drops of green dye in water— changed me. And changed him. One can't change without changing the other. Right?

I tell my counselor I trust deep meaning can emerge from X but I need a guide who can help me see beyond the visible.

TRUTH. I don't realize yet that I've been changed all the way down to the cellular level and I need to relearn myself.
TRUTH. I don't know yet that my guide is in me.

I ask the counselor what I should call him, the jaguar man with no name.

She doesn't have an answer. She suggests she see me once a week for at least six weeks. I agree.

SIXTEEN

I sit in another church with a different friend, one who used to be Catholic like me, before she got fed up, like me. This church is based on universal principles, the power of thought, and quiet meditation before energetic chants. There's no mass, procession, wine and bread symbolizing body and blood, no kneeling and bowing my head, no asking for forgiveness, no disappointed God. People are happy, they smile and hug, and I glare at how fake they must be; their happiness can't be real. Tears well in my eyes, but I push them back. A lady with tissues keeps passing. It annoys me that this church is prepared for my tears. Something churns inside me, and I tighten so I won't explode.

The reverend at this church seems authentic in his love for God, unforced, easy. He preaches for a long time and somewhere inside his sermon everyone else in the congregation evaporates, even my friend, and he preaches directly to me.

He says look at the trees, the ocean, the stars, and I'll see myself. All the power of a star is in me. All the earth's joy is in me. God is in all things, despite appearances. He says challenges press our boundaries so we can be bigger than we ever thought we could be. He says every obstacle is an opportunity to develop a quality that's not yet actualized. I can give myself permission to be strong, even if the world expects me to be broken. Obstacles can lead to blessings. The reverend says something in me wants to be birthed.

FACT. A star is hot gas bound together by its own force of gravity with internal burning and exploding and external pressure trying to make the star collapse. This balance keeps the star alive.

He speaks so quickly I can't capture all his words, but I pull out the words I need most. The reverend preaches that life is good, despite circumstances. Even if there's an appearance of disease or pain, God is still love. No matter what I've done in my life, God is love. No matter what's been done to me, God is love. Gratitude for all things will open the way for something new to occur.

Suddenly, anger like hot lava sears through my veins. No matter what's been done, God is love? My challenges are blessings? I feel myself crack and for the first time I'm angry X happened at all. Why couldn't I just have a nice trip? Why couldn't I spend two weeks falling in love? If life is trying to birth a new quality in me, there are better ways to get my attention. God's greedy mouth bit down on me too hard.

I'm mad at you, I tell God.

It's all right, God says inside my mind.

It's not all right. Tears of rage and a fury of knives tap into my skin. The lady with tissues walks by, and I ignore her.

Our relationship can't survive this, I tell God.

It can, God says.

I clench my jaw. Where were you? I challenge God. Watching? Was it entertaining?

A scream enters my throat. I scream inside my mind while all around me people are clapping.

You could have stopped him, I accuse God. You play too big, I yell at God. Do you hate me? The words are thick and mean. Are you punishing me?

The reverend leads an ovation for God. I refuse to stand. My animosity makes me deaf. I hate these people silently clapping. I hate the reverend mouthing words about God, blah, blah, blah. I hate God.

Do you love him? I spit at God. Do you love the jaguar man?

Yes, God says.

Do you love him more than me?

My joints scream, the church applauds, the reverend prays, and I'm mind to mind with this God who whispers back a drastic truth, I love you both the same.

You love us both the same?

I love you both the same.

MYTH. A jaguar's rosettes light up like stars, the sky looking back at itself.

In that instant I turn off God. I don't mind if God loves the jaguar man a little bit. Even I showed the jaguar man love. But God should love me more. The sun and moon should shine more on me. I manage to control my outward appearance but inside I come completely undone. My thoughts collapse, doors of my mind shake off their hinges, an internal earthquake, a release of tectonic stress along my fault line. I realize if I'm going to understand X from a larger perspective, I'll need a new understanding of love. But I don't know how to do this and even if I had a guide only part of me is willing. Love has gotten too close. Love is trespassing now in my life, pushing me too far, too fast, violently shaking my earth's crust. I think if I can make it through the service I can walk out the church and never come back. The congregation settles back in their seats. My friend hands me a tissue.

Someone sings, the reverend prays, time runs forward and backward. The reverend ends the service, and people file out. The reverend stands at a receiving line, but I walk right by him, turn into the bookstore with my friend. The bookstore has hundreds of books. Some of them would probably help me, but I'm overwhelmed by the choices so I look at a rack of greeting cards and try to calm the temblors in my mind. I walk out the bookstore back into the hallway, which has cleared. Two people remain in the reverend's receiving line. On impulse I join the line. My friend follows and stands beside me. I ask her what I should say. She tells me to say whatever I want. I step out of line. I have nothing to say. She asks if I'm sure. I step back into line and now it's my turn, no time to think. The reverend asks how I am. I say fine and ask him if he takes appointments. He says sometimes he does, but usually he has practitioners who meet with people. I nod my head but don't say anything. I figured he'd say no, another preacher too busy to help, and anyway I don't care, I'll probably never be back.

Why, he wants to know, what's going on?

I bluntly tell him two weeks ago, X, and I'm really mad—I pause for emphasis—at God.

He says he'll meet with me. He turns to his assistant and tells her to set up an appointment with me this week.

All the muscles in my face I've been contracting soften. I say thank you and tears release so freely I can't control their volume or speed. He'll see me. I notice a tiny sense of pride. My problem is big enough for the reverend to see me. The reverend who doesn't take appointments. The reverend who knows how to love. This reverend who didn't flinch when I said X; he'll meet with me this week. *Thank you,* I say inside my fractured mind. *Thank you, thank you, thank you.*

SEVENTEEN

The story of X isn't about X. It is but it isn't. It's about parts and pieces. Yes and no. Big and tiny, jagged and smooth, questions and answers, ahead and behind. Him plus me.

The story of X becomes my story about his story. My focus is on him. There's danger in my focus. The jaguar man and I become constant companions. He's already been stuck inside me, taking up space, but I make more room for him. He moves in. I think I can tame him if I know where he is. I think I can figure him out. So I study him carefully through the door of the internal cage where I keep him. My body becomes heavy with his weight. Distorted.

FACT. A male jaguar can weigh 200 pounds.

SOUVENIR SNAPSHOT. Jaguar locked in a cage with a pig used as bait.

I pretend I'm in control, rational, measured, but actually I'm thinking in circles, a spinning top that's bound to topple.

FACT. If you try to rotate a spinning top in a direction it's not already moving, it will wobble off in an entirely new direction until its inevitable crash.

My crash comes the night of a full moon. I'm looking at the moon, talking on the phone with the diver who's sitting under the same moon countries away. It would be romantic except the diver is lying to me about another woman. I know it, and he knows it.

FACT. Jaguars cover an enormous territory, marking it with urine and scratches on the ground and trees. Their tracks are unmistakable.

I tell him, please don't lie, whatever you do, don't lie. He defends the lie. I defend the truth. He defends himself. The sound of the diver's sweet voice mixes with his lie. The diver mixes with the jaguar man, and I feel myself winding up for a fall. I hang up the phone, drop on my bed, and stare at the light on the ceiling as if it were the moon. I'm spinning, staring at the light, spinning and spinning on a slippery surface, a spinning top making wide uncontrollable sideways loops.

I want the diver to love me, to see that I need to be hugged, to recognize that underneath my strength is fear and under the fear is darkness or emptiness or both. I want him to tell the truth. I want him to get a travel visa, do whatever it takes to come to me. I think a hug, the circumference of embrace, would fix things but I'm alone in my house. There's no one to steady me around the parts that are crashing, and I'm skidding out. I don't even try to hold myself together, tears come, sobs, uncontrollable. I'm perfectly still on the bed but I'm out of control, crashing, falling, crashing, falling, as the bed splits in two, the floor divides, and I fall into a pit, the darkness of grief.

As I'm falling the jaguar man tells me, Sit up straight with your hands visible on your knees.

She stirs.

I don't move. My rational mind knows he's not here.

Sit up . . . Sit up.

No.

The first time I've said no. Who says no? Me or *her*?

Once I say it, I can't stop. NO. I inwardly scream. NO. I silently scream and keep screaming. All the screams I've been holding in, I release them now without sound. He's there, to the right. NO. His touch. GET AWAY. He surrounds me, thick and mean. NO. He's behind me, on my back, at the spot where he held her waistband. NO. He lays a hand on my hair. NO. Emotion bites her with sharp teeth, spits me out in different directions. He seeps out from my pores. He's everywhere I am, she is, the three of us unbearably connected.

I don't want to be here. I don't want to be *her*. I want to claw out of this hole, creep up a tree, take a bite of the sky, morph like clouds into a hundred forms: an ancient elder with legs of a gazelle, a fish head on a plate, or a woodpecker with sharp hooks on its tongue. I want to reach out and grab a wind stream or a dying star. I don't care where it takes me, anywhere out of here.

It's *her* fault. I want her dead.

I want her dead.

I press her further down into the pit. She can't breathe, her lungs compress. She's in too deep and she gags on the sad mud of the earth.

EIGHTEEN

After work I drive in stop-and-go traffic all the way across town to get to my appointment with the reverend. His office is masculine with dark wood, intelligent tones, statues, carvings, and books. The air, furniture, and rug are saturated with incense. I immediately feel calmer as I sit in one of the two leather chairs. The reverend sits next to me, looks at me intently, and says hello. The way he says hello makes me cry. His hello sounds like, "I'm glad you're here." Sounds like, "I want to help. You're going to be okay." Hello, I say back, embarrassed that I'm already crying. I've been crying a lot lately, tears that seem to belong to someone else. The reverend says he wants to meet with me today, but then he'll recommend one of his best practitioners to counsel me. I thank him.

I feel unfocused, my mind a sheet blowing on a clothesline. The reverend tells me he's counseled people on both sides of this issue. He looks me in the eye. The wind calms, and my mind settles. I know I'm in good hands. He's not afraid. I like him for this. I accept the tissue he offers and thank him for telling me that. He asks if I'm ready to pray in. I don't know what that means, but I say yes. I'm ready for whatever comes next.

He takes a deep breath, and so do I. He closes his eyes, and so I do. He prays a long prayer, calls forth the joy, peace, and safety of my life, announces this and that, says God and love and God. My mind doesn't follow the prayer, but it feels good in my heart, and the blood running through my veins starts to energize me, my lungs breathe more deeply, the tight clamps binding my muscles turn a notch toward release.

The reverend wants to hear my story but first he tells me there's part of me that can never be hurt or harmed. I'm as whole now as I was before X. I rummage in my purse for paper and pen and write, "There's part of me that can't be harmed." I tell the reverend about the jaguar man, how I don't think my life can be the same as it was before. He says good. It's time for a new life. I write, "It's time for a new life." He says it's like being a chicken in an egg, praying for a little more room in the egg. No, no, no, no, no. The chicken doesn't realize there's a whole new world outside the egg. I'm like the chicken, he tells me. There's a new way of seeing the world available to me.

Are you willing? he asks.

Maybe, I tell him.

He says it won't always feel good, but it will begin to feel spectacular. I write, "I won't always feel bad."

I tell him about the lights from the bus, lights with no noise coming from the sea, shining on me the instant the jaguar man turned the edge of his knife against my throat. I tell him my prayer: God. One word that filled every cell of my body. God.

He says that's powerful. I ask him what they were, the lights. A bus can't come from the sea. Even if it wasn't a bus, the timing was perfect. The lights appeared, and the moment the jaguar man lowered the knife the lights disappeared.

What do you think they are? he asks me.

I'm shy to say it, in case I'm wrong, but there's an energy of total truth in this office so I look at him and hesitantly tell him what I suspect.

The lights were a miracle?

I want him to say yes or no, it was a miracle or it wasn't. He says a miracle is an instant demonstration of truth, an instant revelation of something that's always going on, though we often can't see it. God is always being God. Love is always being love. Energy is always being energy. Love has no limits. When love is being love sometimes it can blow our minds, especially if we're in the habit of thinking small. The lame walk. The blind see. Lights of a bus emerge from the sea. Some people say a miracle is God doing something out of the ordinary. In reality life is always being life, the difference is we get in tune with what is always happening, we get plugged in, we get aligned with the unlimited power and energy of the universe, and in that moment we know things we didn't know before. We experience a demonstration of healing that in fact was always possible.

So it was a miracle? I wonder.

The reverend says I experienced a sudden loss, something unexpected happened. I was in the jungle and what I thought I knew was torn away. The rules shifted, my old rules didn't apply. That sudden loss moved me to a deep state of emptiness. In that emptiness, I held my attention on God. I allowed the emptiness to be a place for love to fill. There was nothing for the universe to do but respond. I call it a miracle because the response was beyond my wildest imagination. The miracle, he tells me, was the instant I came into alignment. At that moment, I was available for a demonstration of truth. I write, "The lights were a demonstration of truth."

The reverend talks with me for two hours. He never checks a clock. His full attention is on me. I tell him how I prayed over the jaguar man, how I felt genuine compassion. He says that was my true nature at work. I saw beyond my circumstances, I saw the goodness, however small, I saw a glimmer of goodness in the man, and wanting him to heal was an incredible act of love.

I explain how I survived without a mark. The branches and thorns didn't scratch; the mosquitoes and sand flies didn't bite. He says what I give away is what I get back. I gave love, and nature wrapped around me like a barrier, a shield.

I tell him how suddenly things with the diver are falling apart, things at work are falling apart. Everything feels like it's falling apart. He tells me that since a new aspect of my nature has been activated, things I used to attract in my life might not be able to stick. I write, "I'm different, and some things won't stick." My relationships, job, and other things may come undone. Let them, he tells me. Don't fight. Don't try to fix anything. Sit in the silence of my soul. I'm going somewhere I've never been before. Hold on. I write, "Hold on." Trust that this is happening for me, not against me. I write, "This is for me not against me."

Think about the butterfly, he tells me. How can the caterpillar imagine the butterfly? It can't but it's compelled to change. It wraps a cocoon around itself and emits a toxin that burns itself into a new shape. I write, "The caterpillar poisons itself." There's pain involved. Part of the caterpillar has to die. I write, "Part of me is dying." It can't stop the process because the force of nature is too great; nature wants the caterpillar to change.

How do I do that? I ask.

Are you willing? he wants to know.

Yes, I say, but it really hurts.

Yes, it hurts. Are you willing?

Yes.

Then that's all you need to know, he explains. You don't have to know how, only what. Healing, that's where you're going. The universe will show you how.

That's a bad answer, I think. *That doesn't make sense.* But he speaks with such conviction it seems impolite to disagree. I want a formula to follow, homework, step-by-step instructions. As if the reverend can read my mind, he suggests the title of two books to read. I write them on my paper and buy them the next day. He encourages me to take a class at the church and learn how to meditate, so I register for the upcoming class. He tells me to visualize myself from the end result. Visualize anything I want to bring into my life so vividly I not only see myself in the new situations, but I feel the emotions of joy, peace, harmony, bliss, safety, health, and prosperity. I think that is a lot to ask for. That is an impossible dream. He says don't limit my sense of what's possible. Don't go to the ocean with a teaspoon. Go with the biggest bucket I can handle. There's plenty to go around. I write, "Imagine the life I really want to live, bucket not spoon."

He goes to his desk, writes his office, home, and cell phone numbers on a piece of paper and offers it to me. His small paper has weight; it grounds me. I fold it and put it in my wallet where I will keep it for two years until I have enough weight of my own that I can transfer the paper to a drawer. I never call his personal numbers but I have them. They're the net below my tightrope walk, the extra oxygen for my dive.

We both sit quietly, a natural pause. It's dark outside. California summer nights are cool, and through the walls I can feel the evening temperature drop. The reverend asks if I'm ready to pray out, do I feel complete? I don't feel complete. I wish I could stay with him but I say I'm ready. I stuff the paper and pen back in my purse. The reverend reminds me his plan was to meet with me today, then recommend one of his best practitioners to counsel me. I say yes and thank him for this session; he's been an enormous help. He tells me that was his plan but he's changed his mind. He wants to continue counseling me personally. I look at him with such pure gratitude I feel my eyes will melt. I want to change. I want to retrain my thoughts. I want to be a butterfly. I want to understand these strange concepts he's introducing to me.

Thank you, I whisper.

I sit up taller in the chair. Now that I know I'm coming back, I feel that I can leave. He smiles.

I like you, I tell him.

The words slip out. I feel silly saying them. They're too simple, I should say something more intelligent, something about his wisdom and generosity, his insights or spirituality.

I like you too, he says.

I smile back. We both take a deep breath, close our eyes. He claims my wholeness. He claims that all my needs are met. Everything to support my transformation is at hand. It's already done. God and I and love are one. Amen. Amen.

NINETEEN

I decide to use the guest bedroom in my house as a meditation room. I paint the walls light lavender but I'm not making much progress with the floor. I'm too tired to pull out the remaining nails. I want the bounty of home renovations to dry up forever. I consider carpet or a big rug, but I'm finding it difficult to make clear decisions. What do I want? What do I want? If I can't make a decision about the floor how am I going to heal my life?

My friend and I go to the fabric district downtown. Los Angeles has one of the largest fabric districts in the country, hundreds of wholesale and retail shops. I'm shopping for fabric I can send to my mother who has offered to sew curtains for the living room. We park at the edge of skid row and walk down the blocks of fabric stores to one we've been to before. It's overwhelming, countless bolts of fabric stacked floor to ceiling, rack after rack, and circular displays of fabrics in patterns, stripes, and solids. Cotton, linen, silk, upholstery fabric, Lycra, pleather, wool, oilcloth, burlap, canvas, felt, flannel, suede, ribbons, thread, buttons, rhinestones, glitter, lace, on and on and on.

And then I see it: the faux fur. I can practically hear the cheesy music of my soundtrack as I'm magnetized across the crowded store. I wind my way between bolts of lesser fabrics until the faux fur and I are only inches apart, breath to breath, nose to nose, eye to eye. I reach out my hand for the first soft touch, walk around the circular rack, trailing my hand over the many furs in white, purple, green, blue, brown, black, animal prints, orange, yellow, and screaming electric fuchsia. I remove the fuchsia bolt from the display and hold it to my chest. I can't stop hugging it. By now my friend has caught up.

Get it, she tells me.

But what will I do with it?

I rub the fur against my cheek and close my eyes. And then an idea, as electric as the fuchsia, hits me. The floor! My friend thinks this is brilliant. I think this is brilliant. I hug the bolt tighter and make my way to the counter where the lady with scissors does the cutting.

I have a general sense of how big the meditation room is so I buy that much in yardage plus some more, figuring I'm probably wrong. I get the fuchsia fur home, unroll it, smooth it out as best I can, and staple gun it to the floor. I have massive amounts of fur left over so when I drag the futon back into the room I cover that with fur, too. I even have a piece that I throw over the back of the futon to use as a blanket. I add a white floor lamp and a low white table. It's ridiculous. It's uterine, a shocking womb. Defiant femininity on pink overdrive. I'm well aware that this is a decision I will one day regret, but it's reversible, and for now I lie in the middle of the room as if on a surrealist beach gazing at the popcorn ceiling stars and stretch my arms over my head like I'm a happy kid making angels in the fuchsia sand.

TWENTY

I buy a ticket to Belize. My counselor is shocked I want to return to Belize after only a couple of months. My family is worried for my safety. My friends don't trust the diver can handle the intensity of everything that's happened. The reverend recommends I get still and quiet and ask myself if this is the best time. The diver says he'll understand if I don't come; he'll keep loving me even if he has to wait. I ignore all of them and in a flurry buy a ticket. I'm adamant about not allowing the jaguar man to ruin my joy of traveling. And I'm determined to wind the clock backward to restake my claim on a vacation in paradise and falling in love beside the Caribbean Sea.

Adults tend to be fearful of getting hurt while diving, the diver says. It comes with growing up. When kids move underwater, they're not thinking of sharks or barracudas.

I fill my thoughts with sand, waves, sun, and romance. My mind refuses to explore the jungle. My memories shut down at the moment the jaguar man reveals the knife in the van. My mind allows only a few flashes of driving fast down that long road, the vaguest image of turning off the road into the depth of night; it clamps down past the log barricade, where the small road leads to the edge of the sea. I can see the forsaken notch of jungle in broad strokes from a far distance, but from my vantage point it appears innocent and peaceful, a place where the wind stirs leaves, where grasshoppers play notes, and lizards and snakes carve paths the way I run my fingers over sand.

I imagine *she* has finally learned to hide in disguise, become what's around her. She probably swims in the water—a fish, a wave, a moving tide. She burrows beneath vines like a miniscule bug. She leans her head against a tree as if she were moss. Yes, she must have adapted by now. She couldn't still need me. She probably swore me off in my betrayal. If I can forget her and ignore the horrible knocking on the inside of me, I'll be fine.

MYTH. My silk cocoon splits and a misshapen butterfly pushes her way out. (There's no way she'd be whole.) She flies in confused circles on one exhausted wing.

I arrive at the Belize international airport, step off the plane into the humid day, the sun, and the welcoming heat. I walk across the tarmac, stand in the customs line.

Purpose of your trip? asks the customs official.

Pleasure.

The customs official notices I was recently here. You must like our country.

Yes.

At this airport I board the twelve-passenger plane that will take me to the tiny village. There are five men with me on the plane. I'm suddenly nervous, heart beating, sticky palms, as I imagine what these men can do to me. Their hands become the jaguar man's hands, their chatter his voice. I put my head against the small window and clutch my backpack on my lap, the same backpack I had with me in the jungle. I force myself to breathe more slowly, visualize myself landing safely and safely arriving at my cabana, safely walking down the narrow main road, safely playing on the beach, swimming safely in the sea, returning safely at the end of my trip.

I land, collect my bag from the cart. The diver is diving with a group of tourists, so he arranged for a taxi to meet me. I say hello to the taxi driver, double check he's the diver's friend, and force myself to sit in front so I don't appear rude. He's a nice man but he wants to stop somewhere along the road to pick something up or drop something off; I don't know which, but I don't like this at all. I notice he has a knife resting on the console. He actually has a *knife* resting on the console! He pulls off the road down a path where three men and a woman wait in front of a house. His musky odor becomes the jaguar man's scent. I'm practically blind from fear. I silently repeat *I'm okay, I'm okay, I'm okay, I'm okay, I'm okay, I'm okay, I'm okay* until the taxi driver returns to the van, thanks me for waiting, and drives me to the cabana. The first thing I do is put on a bikini and dive into the sea. Its warmth cools my fear, and I float.

The diver meets me after work. He hugs me and hugs me, and I know I've done the right thing coming here. The diver is sweet. I let myself fall in love exactly the way I wanted. I fall in love with the diver, the village, the air, the sea, the sand, and the sun and moon taking turns in the sky. I don't think about *her* stranded only miles down the unpaved road. Nothing interrupts my focus.

FACT. When met with a poisonous snake in the rain forest, give it ample room. If you attempt to scare it, it could attack.

I return a second time to the tiny village to visit the diver. The first time he was sweet, but the second time I catch him in another lie. I discover a girlfriend from a European country visits him in the tiny village. I feel foolish, cliché. I try to be casual—what did I expect—he can see other people but please don't lie. He swears I'm the only one he loves. He twists his story into an almost believable tale, and my head spins it into a story of how everything ends up the way I want. He tries to be sweet, and I try to let the days go by without extending the fight.

Walking back from the beach one day alone, I think I see the jaguar man on the sidewalk but I'm not sure. How can I not remember what he looks like? *Try to remember.* Nails pulled out of wood? No he doesn't. An animal in the tropical forest, a jaguar, lean and fast? No he doesn't. I remember a television show I saw about the ocean. There's an eel in the show, long, thick, fanged. He looks like an eel. No he doesn't. I'm fed up with my own resistance.

Does *she* remember?

SOUVENIR SNAPSHOT. An eel, its serpent head, teeth, and jaw, emerges from behind hard stony coral.

The man on the narrow sidewalk in the tiny village wears a blue bandana. My heart pounds. What color was the jaguar man's bandana? It was red or blue, I can't remember. I walk by, he calls out, Hey girl, you've been here before!

I say yes and walk faster. I tell the diver. He remembers what the jaguar man looks like, tells me not to worry; he's not in this village. I feel better, but what if the diver is wrong, what if he's lying about this, too? I get on the plane to go home and swear I'll never return, not to the diver's lies and a phantom jaguar man lurking on the sidewalk.

FACT. Even if you use a machete to slice a poisonous snake, the decapitated head can chase you and is capable of a venomous bite.

After the visit to Belize, there are phone calls and emails, and the diver is sweet again, making everything seem lovely. I return to the tiny village a third time to visit the diver, but I'm tired. This isn't the kind of relationship I want. I keep an eye out for the jaguar man on the sidewalk. I fantasize that he apologizes, but I'm scared to see him. I don't go to the jungle. I don't want to find *her*.

FACT. Snakes may often remain in your path. (Retreat!)

I return to the tiny village four times to visit the diver. The fourth time he's sweet, but there's a shift in tone. We're both tired. I want to explore the peninsula but I'm nervous to go far, so I swim and walk and wait for the diver to get off work. I consider looking for *her*. The diver refuses to go to the jungle with me; I'll have to go alone. Where would I even begin? I put aside the thought and concentrate on swimming and snorkeling. The moon is full, and there's no sign of the jaguar man on the narrow road.

I reflect on the changes in my life. So many blessings have appeared, without effort. My second round of medical results came back negative. My home is looking good. I meditate daily. The parts of my life I care about, but don't obsess over, are flowing. The parts I'm determined to control don't have the same ease. I want to include the diver more in my life. He says maybe. If it's meant to be, it will be. Maybe he'll join me in Los Angeles. Maybe I'll move to the tiny village. He lets out a single thread of possibility, which I knit into my lifeline. I want his love to stabilize me, but it's getting harder to fool myself. I have to work at it doubly hard, and I'm only half-heartedly committed to the illusion. I'm at odds with myself constantly. I leave the tiny village, go home, and negotiate with myself. The diver will have to visit me next. I'll continue loving him but I'm finished going there.

FACT. Snakes are reptiles. Eels are fish. They're both serpentine but they're not related.

SOUVENIR SNAPSHOT. An eel's twisting body caught in a net.

The diver gets a visa. I think *finally*. I downplay the fact that his main purpose is to visit family in Florida. Still, he says he'd like to see me so I make it happen. We have a brief vacation tucked away from family and friends. Our visit is strained. It's glaringly obvious our lifestyles are too dissimilar to merge, and our relationship has run its course. I swing along a continuum of acceptance, indifference, and panic. He returns to Belize. I tell myself to let go of him and his country, but I'm not as strong as my word. I don't realize yet that I've been spinning a web around him when I should be searching for *her*. The mixed-up part of me still hopes if I can grasp his love and force-feed it until it grows, then I can use his love, like cotton in an old rag doll, to fill the part of me *she* left empty. So I visit the diver in the tiny village a fifth time. There's torrential rain. The diver drinks with buddies while I wait for him in my cabana. When he finally arrives, late in the night, the diver says he's outgrown our visits. I want to be angry, humiliated, but even in my tears I'm relieved. Finally he won't play along, and I have to stop.

I wake up early on my last day in the village, get dressed, and walk down the narrowest main street in the world. The diver is at work. We've already said goodbye. I might not return here for a long time, if ever, and my heart feels like a boat in a storm. I weave across the sand between houses on raised stilts until I reach the small building where I never thought I'd go.

I wait until the man on duty hangs up the phone. He motions for me to sit in the hard chair that faces his desk. He asks how he can help. I tell him I want to report X.

When did it happen? Why didn't I report it immediately? Description of the man. Creole or Mestizo? If I can't give a description, how will he be caught? Where was I? Where on the road? Does anyone else know? Was I traveling alone? The officer looks me in the eye. Am I traveling alone now?

He asks where I'm staying. I wonder why he wants to know where I'm staying and if I'm staying alone. He looks me up and down. I don't trust this officer. He says he takes X very seriously, but in my mind I see him pounce. Fear breeds suspicion; what is he (what is any man) capable of? I begin to cry. I say I changed my mind. I'm not going to finish the report. I tell the officer I'll think about it and maybe come back. But I already know I won't. There's no one in this tiny village to watch out for me, why would I tie a knot to this place now?

MYTH. The world is taking care of the jaguar man. However that plays out, dead or alive, he's receiving his due. It's natural law.

SOUVENIR SNAPSHOT. An old, emaciated jaguar with broken teeth lies on its side in tall grass.

MYTH. The story of X is underneath X. Maybe the jaguar man asks for help and help arrives. He makes amends. Has no victims or enemies. He grows beyond who he was when he was capable of X. Hugs his son, papa's big boy. He's a good father. He's a good father. He's a jaguar boxing paw to paw with his cub.

I step outside, and the sun stuns me.

I squint and walk across the sand. Behind me a voice says, Hey girl, you've been here before!

I spin around and face a smiling man. I don't recognize him. I've never seen him.

You've been here before, he repeats.

He doesn't look like the man who said it three visits ago, but maybe he is the same man. Yes, I say.

He says my name with a question mark. Right?

How do you know my name?

I met you before, he says.

I don't know this man. I've never met him. I'm sure. This man is wearing a bandana; his hair is long dreadlocks. I stare at him, is this the jaguar man? The jaguar man had straight black hair, didn't he? This man is Creole, the jaguar man wasn't Creole, was he? How does he know my name?

When did I meet you? I ask.

I don't remember, he says. I smoke a lot, but I didn't forget your name.

He smiles. He has a dead front tooth. Something deep inside me recognizes the tooth. I don't remember if the jaguar man had a dead tooth, but now that tooth reverberates through my body. He holds out his hand.

It's good to see you again, he says.

I shake his hand. I know that hand. I recognize the feel of that hand. My flip-flops sink in quicksand. My fingers send electric shocks up my arm. My eyes squint in the sun. My mouth politely says, "It's good to see you, too." My brain says, "Get out of here now." I back away, the man in the bandana smiles and laughs and carries a bucket through the sun-streaked blur of a wooden doorway.

I run straight to my cabana to catch my breath on the porch chair. I close my eyes and see the tooth. I go as far back into memory as I can, searching for the tooth, but I can't find it hidden anywhere.

The jaguar man is still inside me. I can feel him in my right hip, like a clog in a passageway. I massage my hip but can't release the pressure. I close my eyes and see the jungle. It's two-dimensional, a paper jungle, origami animals, folded trees, a flat sky. I have to get *her* out of there. I may never return to this tiny village. It's now or never, she needs me. It suddenly feels urgent. But how?

TRUTH. I don't realize how simple (not easy) it is.

MISTAKE. I think she's there and I'm here. I think there's distance.

TRUTH. She isn't in the jungle.

She isn't in the jungle?
The jungle is in me.
The jungle is in me?
These thoughts come to me, fuzzy at first, like fog or clouds or the skin of a peach around its meat. I stare beyond the sea into my past and through my future until I circle back to now.

If I'm going to merge my two halves into a whole, I have to clear away the vines and roots. In me. I have to accept I know what she knows, feel what she feels, am who she is.

I feel what she feels? I am who she is?

TRUTH. I am who she is.

TRUTH. Circumstances don't have to be different before I find my way. How it is *is* the way.

TRUTH. An elegant wholeness can come.

TWENTY-ONE

An elegant wholeness can come.

You start by sitting on the wooden cabana floor, folding paper into grasshoppers and trees and sand and waves. It's confusing. Even as you do it, it's hard for you to understand. You don't know anything about origami, you fold without a plan or vision, and the first grasshopper comes out lopsided, like you. It's a crumple of paper but it must know what you mean because when you place it on the ground it snaps its hind wings and makes a cry that sounds like crackling. It's not a conscious decision to fold a grasshopper, you can't explain why you're doing it, except you feel pulled, like you're a small dog and a great big leash is tight telling you go here, do this. But instead of the yank being around your neck, it's around the empty space inside you, the space that emptied when you left her in the jungle. *Fend for yourself. I don't want you.* You know you'll have to keep going until you find her, even though you can't imagine how big a job this folding is going to be.

You admit you left her on purpose, in a delirium of birdcalls, fish scales, branches, berries, sand flies, stench, snake eyes, jellyfish, feathered tails, and hollowness. You took the physical brunt of the jaguar man while she held the fear. You admit you didn't try to comfort her. You didn't like her anymore.

That may or may not be true. Maybe you like her, maybe you don't. Either way . . . *she knows too much. She knows his knife pressed on her stomach, its sweep across her breast, its pointed play with the strings of her bikini; she knows the smell of his hair, his nauseating breath stuck to the lining of her throat; she knows him pounding her, a hammer to a nail; she knows sharp, insistent, metal, bile. She knows too much. She knows the neutrality of nature, grasshoppers flitting in clumps of tall grass by her knees, the agonizing repetition of the sea reaching forward and pulling back; she knows ugly; she knows acquiescence and commands; she knows the urge to turn the tables, plunge his knife into his chest, carve him like a turkey, slow and steady, then pick his carcass clean. If you're going to accept her, you'll have to accept what she knows.*

After the first grasshopper you can't stop folding, and every grasshopper you place on the floor seems to cry out in fear. Fear hopping. Fear rubbing its long hind legs. Fear breathing through spiracles. One fold follows another. You fold and crease and shape grasshoppers, trees, seaweed, and the waxing moon, shimmering on the deserted surface of the sea. You fold a multitude of forms and you don't know where they're coming from, except maybe they're what she remembers too.

You recreate the jungle with folded thorns, poisonous weeds, sand and shells, and moss as thick and heavy as a cluster of sleeping butterflies. Some of your creations look natural, some take on a new form. You don't think about it and fold according to the pull that keeps pulling you—fold, fold, fold.

You fold the jaguar man into a jaguar, sharp teeth and powerful jaws, a commander of the night. If you could avoid folding him you would, but you need him to find her. You fold his rusted van until it's so small it fits on your fingertip, and the seat in the front is the size of a seed. You fold the road into a snake, then fold the diagonal log barricade he pushed aside. You fold the jaguar man's knife, transform it into a frond of a palm tree, still sharp but not a knife. You fold the darkness of that night into shapes without names, shapes you can't repeat. You fold the jaguar man's anger into lizards that catch grasshoppers in their teeth when you place them on the growing jungle floor.

FACT. Nature has an intricate way of folding and unfolding itself in perfect balance.

Your jungle grows so alarmingly big you know it will consume you soon and you'll come face to face with her. You try to stop folding, but the leash . . .

The jungle becomes saturated. The folded water takes on the scent of salt, and the ground dampens with dew. You fold so many vines that they creep uninhibited up the jungle walls and hang down from the canopy like a curtain on a strange stage. Vines wrap around your legs. It feels as if the vines invade you, filling the space between your muscles and bones with little mediocre thoughts of how you escaped without her. The jaguar man's musk ripens and thickens into a solid paper mass at the base of a gnarled tree.

The jaguar man begins to take over the origami jungle with the same force he took over that night. His breath rises out of the sea like steam. He scuttles along the sand on crab legs. He buzzes his insect wings. He becomes many and all, letter and number, word and thought, high and low. You know if you keep folding he will lead you to her; he will sniff her out. You wonder where she's hiding, what she's been eating, if she's adapted to being alone, if she's wrinkled by water and changed by time, if she's grown scales and thousands of legs, built a fortress, had nightmares of nonsense, forgotten her childhood, or pierced the gods with needle and string.

You wonder if she hates you like you hate her. That's not true. *You hate that you left her. You're ashamed. You protected yourself at her expense. You don't want to see what the jaguar man did to her and what she's become. You do, but you don't.*

The jungle grows and grows like an elaborate excuse. It seems hard to imagine, but your fingertips take on the properties of vines, slippery in the dampness, and it becomes hard to fold with any certainty. Shapes fall into folded chaos, and you swear you hear a flutter of butterflies waking up and beating the sorrowful air with forgiving wings.

Then for the first time the leash stops tugging you from folding, that task paused. You lean back against a rough-skinned tree and feel the layers of jungle shudder. You can sense she's near which means the jaguar man is near too, ready. You're afraid of them both.

You listen for his deep chesty cough. You know what she's in for, and your mind can't wrap around the possibility of living through it twice. Does she want you to watch, like she had to watch?

FACT. Watching something happen changes the way it happens. The more you observe, the greater the effect.

You let your mind click. Click. Your mind drifts away from her and meanders until it catches on an article you read once about a girl and lions in Ethiopia. The girl was twelve and a man wanted to marry her. The girl didn't want to, of course, she was twelve, so the man got six friends and they kidnapped her, took her to a forest and beat her to make her agree to marry him, which is exactly the kind of low-level plan that forges an incredible sense of cosmic grief. Then three growling lions appeared, chased off the men, and surrounded the crying girl whose call for help clearly translated across species. When the police finally found the girl, the lions didn't attack the policemen, instead they walked away into the forest, their job done, and the police took the girl home. Some people, especially scientists, don't believe the story is true.

You've always wanted to be a true believer, the kind who lives by the glad surprise and has faith that in every bad situation there's an inherent fold in reality and logic big enough for a lion to pass through. Still, the girl in Ethiopia paid a price too high.

Leaning against a tree's shoulder, you look for your own opening. You can no longer make sense of place and space. It occurs to you that if she has already found an escape then you're here by mistake.

You stand up. A rustle in the leaves. You turn around. The musk of the man. Things change from this to that. The tree becomes the leather strap he used to wrap your wrists. A dragonfly sprouts beetle legs that will not run. A fish takes on a tail of a bird that looks like the curve of the hat you wore.

Grasshoppers crawl across your toes and up your legs. The jaguar man creeps beside you. From the sheer will to protect yourself, you furiously flatten a chunk of the paper sea into an armor plate then wait for his attack on you or her, you don't know which, but the jaguar man remains crouched between thorny branches. The anticipation builds up a panic in you that makes you feel as if you're drowning in the armor. The place in your body where screams are made is clogged with dread and seaweed.

You wonder if the girl in Ethiopia screamed. You wonder how many girls and women around the world scream or don't scream. You fold a scream, and it drops like a shell to the bottom of the sea.

There is nowhere to go, and you can't risk the jaguar man coming for you or her, taking you with one crushing bite. You close your eyes and call her once. You keep your eyes closed when you call but you feel a breeze against your chest. It's either her coming to you or it isn't. You pull with your teeth at the vines on your fingers until you loosen the vines and your fingers can bend.

You begin at your toes and fold them upward and over, then down and away, accordion style. Your hands are stiff but you manage to move up your legs, folding your legs along with whatever is stuck to them, salt and sand. You crease the edges with the heel of your hand to make sure the folds hold place. You fold yourself into a story.

You fold up your chest, and it's true you don't check to see if she's there although you feel a brushing of wings or a tapping as if on a door you might want to enter. Then a deep breath, like wind from an ancient place, enters your body. You get the sensation of two friends sitting uncomfortably side-by-side, or maybe they're generous or shy. It's hard to describe things you're still figuring out.

You keep folding along one arm, then your neck and head. You fold yourself into a sentence. You fold down the other arm to your final two fingers. You fold yourself into a single word that keeps changing.

X means compassion (for you and her).

For all the things I've done well, and all the things I haven't.

X means love.

So big I have to change my life to comprehend it.

You fold yourself until there's no she or you or him, no here and there, no jungle or sea, or jaguar or God. Until you're all and none.

I used to be one person and then I was more. I, we, drifted in the water, bumping up against the shore, until we got caught on this vine of past and present and stayed here twisted on each other as the night shaped itself into morning.

MYTH. The end of the world, and the beginning of a new one, will come when a jaguar climbs up a vine into the sky and devours the stars and the moon.